The Nor'Westers

The Nor'Westers
The Fight for the Fur Trade

Marjorie Wilkins Campbell

FIFTH
HOUSE

Interior and Cover Design by Mark Shaver / Icon Communications
Front cover painting by Frances Anne Hopkins, courtesy National Archives of
Canada, C–002774
Map illustrated by Toby Foord

The publisher gratefully acknowledges the support of The Canada Council for the
Arts and the Department of Canadian Heritage. We acknowledge the financial sup-
port of the Government of Canada through the Book Publishing Industry
Development Program for our publishing activities.

Printed in Canada by Transcontinental

02 03 04 05 06 / 5 4 3 2 1
First published in the United States in 2002

NATIONAL LIBRARY OF CANADA CATALOGUING IN PUBLICATION DATA

Campbell, Marjorie Wilkins, 1902–1986
  The Nor'westers

  Includes index.
  ISBN 1-894004-97-3

  1. North West Company—History—Juvenile literature.
  2. Fur trade—Canada—History—Juvenile literature. I. Title.
FC3212.3.C35 2002   380.1'4397'097109033   C2002-910776-8
F1060.7.C19 2002

Fifth House Ltd.   In the United States:
A Fitzhenry & Whiteside Company   Fitzhenry & Whiteside
1511-1800 4 St. SW   121 Harvard Avenue, Suite 2
Calgary, Alberta, Canada   Allston, MA 02134
T2S 2S5

1-800-387-9776

Contents

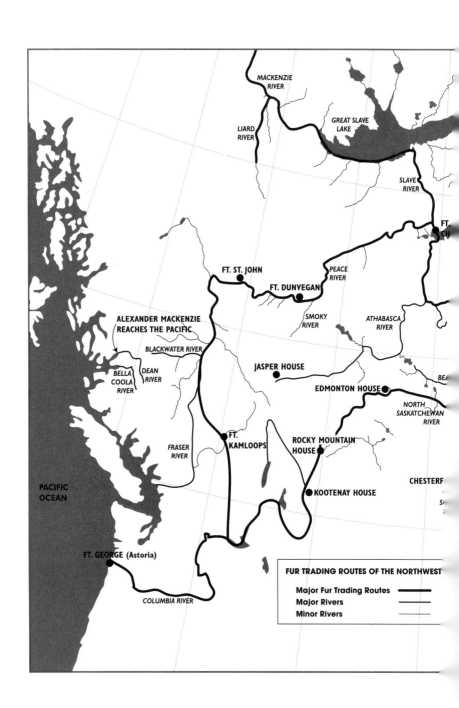

MACKENZIE RIVER

GREAT SLAVE LAKE

LIARD RIVER

SLAVE RIVER

FT. CH

FT. ST. JOHN

PEACE RIVER

FT. DUNVEGAN

SMOKY RIVER

ATHABASCA RIVER

ALEXANDER MACKENZIE REACHES THE PACIFIC

BLACKWATER RIVER

BELLA COOLA RIVER

DEAN RIVER

JASPER HOUSE

EDMONTON HOUSE

BEA

NORTH SASKATCHEWAN RIVER

FRASER RIVER

FT. KAMLOOPS

ROCKY MOUNTAIN HOUSE

PACIFIC OCEAN

CHESTERF

S

KOOTENAY HOUSE

FT. GEORGE (Astoria)

COLUMBIA RIVER

FUR TRADING ROUTES OF THE NORTHWEST

Major Fur Trading Routes	———
Major Rivers	——
Minor Rivers	—

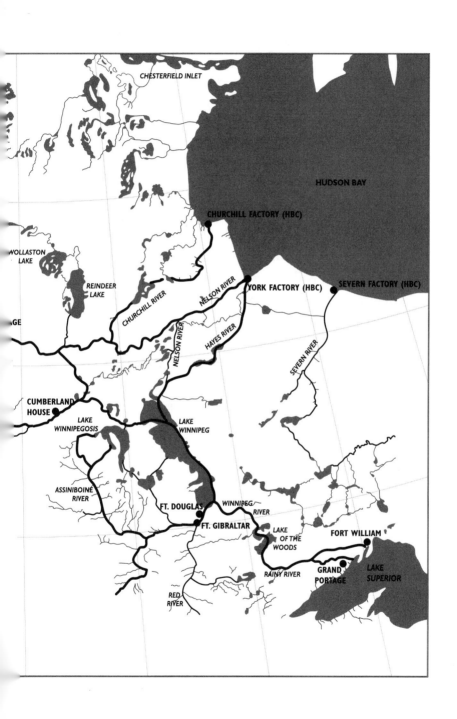

Foreword

When considering history books, people often wonder how writers can write stories about pasts they have not witnessed. One answer is by reading what was written at the time. Reading the works of scholars is another. But it's more than that, too. Above all you must imagine, intensely, until the pictures built of words strike the reader with the same buzz that reality does. This is what Marjorie Wilkins Campbell achieved in *The Nor'Westers*.

Part of projecting into the past is knowing the landscape. Long before Ms. Wilkins Campbell was an accomplished journalist and writer in Toronto, she was a farm girl on a Qu'Appelle Valley homestead. The landscapes of childhood are hard wired into us, and Ms. Wilkins Campbell's understanding of places the fur traders and explorers had travelled is a great strength.

The Nor'Westers is a chronicle of the first attempt by a Canadian company to go head-to-head against an older, richer foreign concern. The upstart was the North West Company; the established business the Hudson's Bay Company, upon which the King of England had bestowed a monopoly. A small operation trying to best a big one must be better than its competition, and in many ways the NWC was better. In the end, the HBC could not win its war with the Nor'Westers and absorbed the company instead. Though the Nor'Wester name was lost, it was far better than defeat. Ms. Wilkins Campbell saw the drama in this story and wrote it as well as anyone has. Thanks to this new edition, one of Canada's most exciting stories will live on.

Fred Stenson

Preface

There are several reasons for the lack of popular accounts of the North West Company. For one thing there are the mechanical difficulties of handling so many leading characters on so vast a stage over nearly fifty years. There is the necessity for introducing a page of our history little known to even the average Canadian reader. But the main difficulty, until recently, has been the lack of reliable information necessary to piece together this remarkable saga of Canadian enterprise. Enough of the facts are now available, thanks to numerous painstaking and imaginative researchers, to tell a fairly comprehensive story.

Many persons and institutions have made possible this short account of the Nor'Westers. I've talked with men and women and visited libraries and historic sites from Montreal to the Peace River and the Pacific slope. Though I am grateful and indebted to hundreds of sympathetic, interested and informed people, I can mention only a few. These must include Miss Mary Grace Hamlyn, Redpath Library, McGill University, all who have in any way contributed to the Champlain Society volumes covering the North West Company and, most of all, Dr. W. Stewart Wallace, chief librarian of the library of the University of Toronto, a worthy scion of the Nor'Westers, if ever there was one.

Marjorie Wilkins Campbell
Toronto, June 1954

The Great Bonanza

*I*n Montreal, in 1779, everyone—and everything—depended on the fur trade. Tall ships brought cargoes of goods from far-off ports in England and France and the West Indies—and sailed away laden with pelts. Low-lying, long canoes carried trade goods to the remote interior of the continent—and returned loaded to the gunwales with bales of beaver and marten, fox, muskrat, and weasel.

For Montreal was the centre, the heart, of the two great operations. From spring until late autumn her harbour throbbed with the coming and going of ships. As soon as each ship anchored, swarms of strong young stevedores boarded her and, like ants, carried off her cargo. Strings of creaking carts bore the cargoes up the rutted streets to the warehouses. They met other strings of creaking carts lurching down to the St. Lawrence River, piled high with furs each year trapped deeper and deeper in the unknown, uncharted continent.

Those great, two-wheeled carts shuttling up and down Montreal's streets were the pulse of the colony's business. The more carts, the more money Montrealers had to spend. Habitants along the river could sell their farm produce. Canoemen could sign on for year-long trips to the Indian country. There were balls in winter. Taverns rang with cheerful banter. In the stores and warehouses, where the air always reeked of the smell of untanned hides, clerks toiled over accounts and the endless packaging of trade goods, and received good wages.

The sound of those creaking carts, the cheery greetings of carters, even the ribald curses of sweating dockhands was music to Montreal. But what if the carts ceased their creaking? What if fewer and fewer canoe-loads of pelts came down from the Indian country?

Most Montrealers, during busy summer months, never even thought of the possibility of the fur trade petering out, like a freshet when the spring run-off had ended. But when winter came they had time for thoughts about the future. And, naturally, the town's more prosperous citizens did most of the thinking about what might happen. They, the merchants, knew that the entire fabric of the fur trade could crack up like a canoe in a churning, white-water rapid.

Simon McTavish thought often during the winter of 1779 that the great fur trade business was very much like a fragile bark canoe caught in a rapid without a competent steersman. Or, more aptly, like a canoe with half a dozen *voyageurs* who each thought he could—and should—steer it. And Simon McTavish was a shrewd young Highland Scot who understood even more of the colony's sole industry than he saw with his quick, wide-set eyes.

Already in the four years since he had made Montreal his headquarters, McTavish had become a familiar figure. On the street men and women turned to admire or envy as he strode proudly about his business. At the handsome houses that were slowly spreading the town toward the wooded slopes of Mount Royal, the girls patted their hair and fluffed out their billowing silken skirts when they saw him at a party. Their merchant fathers eagerly accepted invitations to supper at his comfortable quarters over his fine new stone warehouse on St. Vincent Street. When he appeared at Dillon's Tavern, the merchants expected more than casual talk over the meat pie and ale and good, nippy cheese. For McTavish's generous mouth tightened to a thin line of determination just as easily as it softened to an engaging smile.

At twenty-nine Simon McTavish was a very successful business man. After a couple of years of forwarding rum from Schenectady for the fur trade at Michilimacinac, he had outfitted several expeditions to the Indian country; in a single season he had taken to London in one of the tall ships pelts worth well over £15,000. Each year now he went up to the inland depot at Grand Portage to send off his own canoe brigade to the northwest. Each year he imported larger consignments of manufactured goods from Europe, more rum from the West Indies. He was an experienced executive and a born leader.

But so, too, were several other merchants then doing business in Montreal. The Yankee trader, Alexander Henry, a portly man in his high white stock and collar, was popular at the gatherings at Dillon's Tavern, though for other reasons. Few men told a better yarn. Old Alexander Henry, they called him, not because he was really old, but because at forty he had had more hair-raising experiences than all the rest of them. When winter froze the St. Lawrence River and the smaller streams that made up the highways of the time, it also isolated the town at the foot of Mount Royal. Entertainment was such as people could make among themselves, and a yarn from Alexander Henry livened many a sober discussion concerning the future of the fur trade for both merchants and their clerks and apprentices.

Henry had been at Michilimacinac when the great Indian chief, Pontiac, had tried to drive the white invaders from his people's ancient hunting-grounds. Following an exhibition lacrosse game Pontiac's warriors stormed the fort gate while the governor and his men were watching the play, and killed over seventy of the garrison. Henry hid under a pile of hides, and with the help of a blood-brother Indian escaped being discovered. He lost all his trade goods. But the next year, 1764, he had formed a partnership with a Frenchman at nearby Sault Ste. Marie, and had headed a highly profitable trade venture into the country southwest of Lake Superior. He had then gone into the northwest with a small group of traders, only to be robbed by a powerful chief, Chatique, on the Saskatchewan River. And on the Saskatchewan he had barely escaped starving to death by chewing on the remains of a red deer killed by wolves and frozen in the river ice. Now, his savings invested in a lucrative merchandising business, he was keenly concerned with the future of the colony's basic industry.

There were, too, the Frobisher brothers, three stocky Yorkshiremen who were a whole business in themselves. Joseph and Thomas had already spent several winters in the northwest. They had travelled up with Alexander Henry, going beyond the Saskatchewan River to the Churchill to found a post at Ile à la Crosse, where they hoped to intercept Indians going to the Hudson's Bay Company's Fort Churchill. They had succeeded handsomely, too. The third brother, Benjamin, remained in Montreal to manage the business end of Frobisher & Company. Like Henry, these three were most enthusiastic about the fur trade of the northwest. They had seen the finest beaver trapped along those distant streams. They sensed the potential riches to be had. But more important, they knew of new streams yet to be discovered and explored. They had heard from the natives of distant shining mountains, and over those mountains a great salt water which must surely be the Pacific Ocean. Some day some man would find a passage across the mountains and a way to the riches of China, the goal for which the starting-point of the long canoe route, La Chine, had been named.

Each man who had been on one of those long exciting trips to the interior, the *pays d'en haut* or up-country, had faced starvation; he had watched against attack by Indians in retaliation for wrongs suffered from the French or English. But what was danger compared with the reward of discovering new country, of making a fortune in a single trip? It was this dual challenge of potential danger and potential wealth, the great bonanza of the northwest, that led merchants to seek means of preventing the disaster that threatened.

The McGill brothers, James and John, had traded in both the southwest country at the headwaters of the Mississippi River, and in the northwest. And there was another Yankee, Peter Pond. Pond, like Henry, had come up to Montreal from New England to seek his fortune, following the conquest of Canada. He had been among the little party attacked by Chief Chatique for several kegs of rum and a small fortune in trade goods. Because game was often scarce on the Lower Saskatchewan, Pond had turned his experience as a supply agent with General Amherst's army to relieving the constant threat of starvation. In his first years in the northwest he made one of the greatest contributions to the entire fur trade—he developed a supply line. Since there was absolutely nothing to eat but game, he persuaded the Indians to trade dried buffalo meat, or pemmican, as well as pelts. And then, to improve on his contribution, he cached bags of the sustaining food along the route rapidly being developed between Montreal and the Churchill River.

These men were well aware of the legacy left them by the French fur-trader explorers, La Vérendrye, Du Lhut, La Salle and Radisson. Long before the close of the French regime these and other Frenchmen had developed a system of trade with the natives. The French had organized canoe routes, and even fixed prices for various pelts. Most important, they had created among the natives a need for manufactured goods, for the Indians found that with arms and ammunition, life was much easier. After the fall of New France the traders who poured into Montreal from the towns along the Hudson River had only to engage experienced French-speaking canoemen or *voyageurs* and guides familiar with the trade routes, and resume the business interrupted by the conquest.

Within a very few years they had the trade back into full swing. By 1779 they had built up more than half a dozen individual prosperous businesses. Each employed clerks and apprentices to repack the blankets and kettles, the arms and shot and beads brought in by the ships, into smaller bales suitable for stowing in a canoe, to siphon barrels of rum into kegs small enough for a man to carry on his back across a portage. And because those merchant-traders were men of initiative and courage they attracted the finest of the French-Canadian canoemen who had been born along the rivers and who were happiest when they got their knees on the bottom of one of the frail craft.

But the very qualities of individual enterprise and courage which had built up Montreal's several lucrative businesses were strangling the whole. They were bringing about the nightmare—

and the very real danger—which Simon McTavish and his fellow merchants feared. To survive as well as make profits in the remote Indian country a man had to be able to take care of himself. He had to be able to make quick decisions and abide by the consequences of those decisions. He must be a leader, and a leader isn't always a good partner.

The trouble with the fur trade in 1779 was that each merchant-trader wanted to be leader. Each was in competition with the others. There was, of course, the Hudson's Bay Company, chartered a hundred years before by Charles II of England, and holding a monopoly to all the country drained by rivers flowing into Hudson Bay. But the Hudson's Bay Company had shown little interest in exploring or developing its monopoly. The French, apart from a local struggle on the northern bay, had shrugged their shoulders and traded with the natives in spite of the English company, and the new Montrealers did exactly the same. Indeed, they co-operated with each other only when on rare occasions in the northwest they found themselves in actual competition with the Hudson's Bay Company.

To reach the richest fur-bearing areas, the wilderness to the northwest of Lake Superior, Montreal traders had to send their trade goods by canoe up the Ottawa River to Lake Nipissing and across Georgian Bay to Lake Superior. From the inland depot at Grand Portage on the west shore of Lake Superior, *voyageurs* carried all their goods up over the height of land, loaded them into smaller canoes and then travelled by Rainy River and the Lake of the Woods to Lake Winnipeg—and beyond. That was costly in itself. Canoemen had to be paid wages, and fed. So had clerks and wintering partners who took charge of each outfit. In addition were the costs of warehousing in Montreal, of clerks and helpers there, and of importing trade goods. Because of all these expenses, many thousands of prime beaver and other pelts must be collected annually if any profit could be shown. Credits were hard to arrange, because each trade venture took three or four years from the time the trade goods were ordered abroad, taken to the interior and the pelts brought out and shipped to the London market for auction.

The combination of high costs and long credits forced each merchant to instruct his wintering partners to get pelts at any cost. Give the Indians more rum, they ordered. Hand out more presents. Deck the Indian girls with more beads, the young men with bright red blankets. So the competition grew. The natives soon realized the actual state of the struggle. With half a dozen individual traders bidding for their trade at every strategic meeting-place, they shopped around to see who would give them most rum, most blankets and beads and arms. The competition was fine for the Indians, but it was quickly ruining the merchants.

McTavish and the Frobishers remembered the 1775 trip. That year, forced by Chatique's plundering, the traders had pooled their goods and as a result had made a profit of some £60,000. Surely a similar pooling of resources would save them all from ruin now. Not all the merchants agreed, however. Some determined to remain free-traders. But finally a small group decided that co-operation was the surest way to keep pelts arriving from the Indian country and ships coming into harbour with trade goods. The Frobishers, Alexander Henry, Peter Pond, the McGills and Simon McTavish formed a company. They pooled their trade goods and capital, and divided the whole into sixteen shares.

It was a radical step for men who had proved that they were individually courageous and enterprising beyond question. For each had his eyes on adventure and the making of a fortune. Indeed, each might well have given the new company his own name, confident of winning control of the great bonanza. Instead, they gave it a name which was in itself a symbol. They called it the North West Company.

2

Pork-Eaters

*E*ach spring, before the last ice was out of the river or the first willows had burst into bud, hundreds of canoemen arrived at Lachine. They came swaggering, smoking their short pipes, dressed in their best shirts and caps, bright sashes a-swing at their waists. In gay, cheery French they greeted one another:

"Ho, Gabriel, so you have married the little Marie!"

"François, you are now steersman, my friend. I am glad."

"You are not afraid of the wolves, young Pierre, on your first trip to Gran' Portage?"

"Bonjour, mon bourgeois!"

Some had signed on at Quebec, some at Three Rivers and Sorel; most came from the farms along the river near Montreal. But each carried on his shoulder the proud symbol of his office—his gaily painted paddle.

In the fur trade each *voyageur* provided his own paddle. His employers bought the canoes. They supplied the tough, sinewy roots or watape and the rolls of birch bark with which he would patch the craft, the pine gum to seal the seams. They found his rations for the trip—two pounds of cornmeal and a little fat pork a day for each man, his blanket and two pairs of trousers and two shirts, and several pounds of carrot-twist tobacco. But a paddle was a personal possession. Not only was it the *voyageur*'s badge of office and his constant companion, but on its toughness his life and that of his companions often depended. It became part of him. Usually it was a link with home, a present from his father who had been a canoeman before him, or fashioned by himself over long winter hours while his thoughts lingered on the girl on the next farm.

He would never become a partner, nor even a clerk. He would be an old man at forty, and forced to retire. But who thought of the effects of exposure and hard toil when he was young? To be on the river, that was what a young man craved. To travel the up-country, to shoot white rapids, to be the strongest man carrying two or even three ninety-pound packs over the longest portage without stopping to rest—that was each *voyageur*'s dream, whether he was a pork-eater or a northman. For the hardy young *Canadiens* who manned the canoes worked in two groups. Those who took the brigades up to Grand Portage and back lived on pounded corn and lard. They were called *mangeurs du lard* by the *hommes du nord* who took over at Grand Portage and who lived on the fish and game and wild rice of the northwest.

Each spring Montreal temporarily transferred its interests eight miles upstream to Lachine at the head of the rapids. There, by early May, the squared timber warehouses were already filled to the rafters with ninety-pound packs of trade goods; supplies for the depots at Michilimacinac, Sault Ste. Marie and Grand Portage; with mountains of kegs of rum. New thirty-six-foot-long canoes, each six feet wide at the middle and capable of carrying four tons, bobbed alongside the rough plank docks.

As the days lengthened and the sun warmed the air, Lachine seemed to spread itself. The noise at the dockside became deafening—*voyageurs* singing or cursing, clerks issuing orders, merchants or *bourgeois* shouting instructions and making final checks to see that all was in good order.

"Careful with that keg . . . that bung, is it sealed? . . . Watch how you stow those bow packs!"

Gradually, one after another, each great canoe was loaded until not a sign of its strong white cedar frame or floor boards could be seen. Into each went, as well as the cargo, provisions for the crew of eight or ten—several hundred pounds of corn, dried and cracked in a lye solution and ground, and kegs of fat pork; each man's forty pounds of personal luggage, which included his blanket and clothes; a kettle and hatchet; towlines, mast and lug sail; a ten-foot pole for use on shallow reaches, and a great oilcloth to protect the cargo in wet weather. And at last the flag on the high prow of the *bourgeois*'s canoe, in the spring of 1779 for the first time a flag bearing the letters of the new North West Company—N. W. Co.

On shore wives and children, sweethearts and parents, and the merchants and clerks who would carry on the fur business in Montreal during the summer called out farewells, *bon voyage*, God bless you! The air was crisp and disturbing with the fragrance of bursting buds. Here and there a young man caught the eyes of a dark-haired girl in the crowd, a young husband smiled an intimate message to his wife. The swollen Ottawa, known sentimentally for decades as the Grand River, flowed strong under each craft. In their places just behind the middle seat the *bourgeois*, on their way to superintend the summer's up-country trade, pressed their high beaver-felt hats tighter on their heads against the strong breeze. Steersmen and bowsmen kneeled in their places for a brief moment, waiting. And then the order rang out, "Away!" Slowly, proudly, the bright paddles rose, flashed in the sun, and dug deep in the rushing, icy water. Steadily each canoe moved off from the landing-stage. Arms rose and fell, rhythmically. The low craft shot forward. Soon the brigade, part of several hundred canoes which would leave during the spring season, was out in the main stream. Space blurred familiar faces on the shore. The last farewells died on the wind.

But the canoes weren't quite on their way yet. Half an hour's steady paddling, and they would stop for a final, eventful ceremony. The *voyageurs* would make their peace at the shrine of Ste. Anne, their patron, commemorated by Sir Thomas Moore in the "Canadian Boat Song":

Faintly as tolls the evening chime,
Our voices keep tune and our oars keep time.
Soon as the woods on the shore grow dim
We'll sing at Ste. Anne's our parting hymn.

Peter Pond on his first trip to the northwest described the rough little log church in his own quaint spelling:

"Heare is a small box with a Hole in the top for ye reseption of a Little Money for the Hole [holy] father or to say a small Mass for those who Put a small Sum in the Box. Scars a Voiger but stops hear and Puts in his mite and by that Meanes they Suppose thay are Protected. While absent the Church is not Locked But the Money Box is well secured from theaves . . ."

The Ottawa River was the great highway between Montreal and the fur trade country beyond. Up it each spring brigade after brigade pressed forward. In the morning *voyageurs* often broke thin ice carefully as they set out before breakfast, the bark prows making a swishing sound as they cut through it; yet by noon the sun was so hot they were glad to shed their shirts. In late summer, when the furs had all been collected, the brigades returned amid the hush of autumn's blaze of colour. The round trip took from four to five months.

Seated comfortably, low in the canoes, the newly organized partners had ample time to mull over plans for their company. For those interested in shipping the pelts to the markets of Europe, particularly Simon McTavish and the Frobisher and McGill brothers, the great stands of tall white pine and spruce ranging far beyond the river's banks were a constant source of reassurance; here was timber for ships to sail the seas of the entire world. And when the gentlemen wearied of plans and long snoozes, their *voyageurs* never tired of entertaining them with the gay songs that paced each strong steady paddle stroke. There were many popular songs, though none more popular than:

En roulant ma boule roulant,
En roulant ma boule.
En roulant ma boule roulant,
En roulant ma boule.

When the *bourgeois* or other passengers wearied of sitting in their cramped seats there would always be a portage not far distant. As the *voyageurs* neared shore, the bowman sprang into the water, no matter how cold; no chance could be taken of a submerged rock or deadhead damaging the frail craft. Steadying the canoe, he waited while the steersman also leapt into the icy water. Then, the two holding it steady, the middlemen stepped overside and each stood while a passenger climbed on his strong shoulders. Riding pick-a-back, the passengers were carried to dry land. While they stretched their legs, strolling up the path beside the rapid, the canoemen dried out as they carried the four tons of cargo and the canoe itself. When the canoe was re-loaded above the rapid, the disembarking procedure was reversed. The steersman waded into the stream, held the craft while the bow-man took his grip on the bow. Again mounted on the shoulders of the middlemen, the passengers returned to their places. For, of course, there were no docks or landing-stages along the route.

There were many places where the canoes had to be carried. Between Montreal and Georgian Bay thirty-six portages and *décharges* necessitated stops. Where the rapids were so swift that the entire cargo had to be removed and carried, as well as the canoe, the stop was known as a portage; if part of the cargo could be left in the canoe while it was hauled over the swift water, the *voyageurs* made what they called a *décharge*.

Day after day they dug their paddles into the swift-flowing Ottawa. Each morning they started at day-break, stopping briefly for breakfast at eight and again at two o'clock for lunch. When dusk fell and the long day was over, each canoe must be unloaded, its cargo carefully stowed and covered before the *voyageurs* lit a fire for their supper of cornmeal boiled with a handful of pork—and a precious tot of rum. Occasionally during the day they had paused for a rest and to light their pipes, and by those pauses they measured the day's journey; it was three pipes, or four pipes, or more. To sleep, they had a choice of lying under the overturned canoe or under the stars. Without undressing, each wrapped himself in his blanket. After fourteen or sixteen hours paddling, even the ground was a welcome bed.

Already there were famous places along the route—the Long

Sault Rapids where Adam Dollard and his seventeen young French companions had lost their lives heading off the Iroquois from attacking Montreal in 1660; the Carillon and Rideau Rapids, and the Chaudière Falls where later the City of Ottawa was to rise. At the Chaudière Falls every canoe had to be unloaded and hauled up by a comparatively safe passage. This stretch was one of the worst on the trip. Within the next five miles the pork-eaters faced ten portages: one every half-mile, on an average. Faces bleeding from mosquito and black-fly bites below the wide band of the tumpline, they trudged forward and back again, forward and back, each trying to carry more and to trudge faster than all the others.

And then, after the Ottawa, the shallow, grey, often storm-tossed Lake Nipissing, and beyond it the French River. For a time now they were travelling with the current instead of bucking it. But as the seven crosses at the Grand Recollet suggested, the French River wasn't all easy. Those seven crosses marked the graves of seven *voyageurs*. At the Grand Recollet it was customary to carry the cargo round the main rapid, and then to reload and shoot the stretch of white water beyond. This was comparatively safe, so long as a couple of strong *voyageurs* guided the craft from the shore with a long, strong rope. The seven took a chance. They tried to shoot the rapid without guide lines from the shore. As soon as the canoe hit the eddy it was sucked under. All seven young men drowned, and the cargo was lost.

After the swift French River, Lake Huron's Georgian Bay looked like a vast ocean of great wind-swept waves. To protect themselves against those waves the superstitious *voyageurs* tossed bits of tobacco and trinkets overboard to appease *La Vieille*, "The old lady", as they called the wind.

"*Souffle, souffle, la vieille!*" they cried.

But the old lady wasn't always in a mood to be appeased. Often squalls of cold rain drenched cargo and men, and then a long stop must be made while the bales were opened and dried, yards and yards of bright printed calico and blankets draped over the surrounding bushes. After such delays, the *bourgeois* urged them to paddle faster, and for longer hours. They scarcely fell asleep beside the camp fire, it seemed, before morning came and the guide woke them with his loud "*Lève! Lève!*"

At Sault Ste. Marie the North West Company eventually built a tiny lock round the rapid to speed the trip and lessen the cost of the long haul on the St. Mary's River. But ahead there was still the vast sweep of Lake Superior. Hugging the north shore the brigade sped finally toward the towering twin rocks that guard the entrance to the Nipigon River, where for generations Indians had painted their families' histories on the rocks and appeased their spirits with gifts of tobacco.

Nipigon was important because the next main stop would be Grand Portage. Short of Thunder Bay the brigade came to Point au Père Jesuit. At Point au Père Jesuit each brigade paused while everyone got ready for the grand arrival at the depot. There each man shaved. The *voyageurs* donned their best shirts and sashes and caps. The *bourgeois* put on their top hats of fine beaver felt, for even they had some interest in the pretty girls who would surely be on hand to greet the brigade.

Then, tense with excitement, the canoemen propelled each canoe over the choppy water with strong, measured thrusts of their paddles. Suddenly they rounded Point au Chapeau. At the head of the shallow bay, in the afternoon shadow of brooding Mount Maud, stood Grand Portage. From its palisaded walls came a welcoming burst of musket fire, a *feu de joie*. Each man's pulse quickened. Each listened eagerly for the first cries of welcome from the crowds rushing down to the shore, the merchants and clerks and stolid Indians, to the excited barking of the dogs. And so, singing a *chanson* whose metre matched each rhythmic, measured paddle stroke, the brigade swept up to the dockside.

3

Grand Portage

*J*ndian bands had led the first French explorers into the little bay guarded by Point au Chapeau and Point à la Framboise on the lake side and by Mount Maud to the west. Probably the first white man to visit here had been Jacques de Noyon, early in the eighteenth century. Even then Grand Portage was a well-established Indian camp-site on the ancient water route that stretched right across North America. It had been named Grand Portage by the French because it was the longest and most difficult carrying-place they had encountered. The French had built its first picket stockade, erected its earliest log shacks.

Now, in 1784, it was an outpost of civilization and trade for the Nor'Westers. Simon McTavish, at thirty-four a leading man in the fur trade, looked at Grand Portage with pride and satisfaction as his hand-picked *voyageurs* swung his great canoe up to the narrow dock. But McTavish's delight over arrival at the depot was as nothing compared with that of his nephew, William McGillivray. McGillivray, a young man of nineteen, recently arrived from Scotland, had been hearing about this great wilderness outpost ever since the brigade left Montreal.

Soon the two were stretching their long legs on the narrow dock. While merchants and clerks and interpreters crowded round to greet McTavish, McGillivray took a quick glance over the site. Immediately in front of them the stockade barred a close view of the depot's buildings, but above it towered the high-pitched roof of the main building, and on either side, a row of lower, high-pitched roofs. Grand Portage! Nothing he had heard quite prepared him for the size of the post. For eleven months of the year, he knew, it was isolated except for a few caretakers and an occasional Indian encampment. But now, in July, there must be several thousand people present. Between the stockade and the Indian tents pitched half a mile or so down the shore, the pork-eaters already arrived from the east had set up their camp, rows of upturned canoes, under which they slept, and rows of cooking fires. Far across a small creek ranged the weathered tents of the northmen, from the northwest, the *hommes du nord* who never missed an excuse to prove their fighting prowess over the pork-eaters; indeed, as McTavish had told his nephew, the camps were separated by the creek to prevent fights, if possible. And winding past the upturned canoes and the weathered northmen's tents stretched a well worn trail, the portage road skirting Mount Maud and leading to the remote, fabled northwest itself. Next year McGillivray himself would follow that trail westward.

But his uncle was introducing him to some of the gentlemen. Joseph Frobisher and Peter Pond had just come down that trail. A tremor of excitement flashed through William as he shook hands with these famous wintering partners; in a strange way he felt himself a link between his handsome, respected uncle and these courageous men who had actually traded with the Indians. The feeling lingered as he followed McTavish toward the stockade gate. He felt at home with the noisy, jostling throng of *voyageurs* bent under their burdens of bales and kegs, of clerks and northmen greeting one another after an absence of many months. Entering the great hall, a lump rose in his throat. For a moment he couldn't speak because of a mixture of gratitude to his uncle for getting him into the fur trade, of excitement over actually being at the very centre of the far-flung trade, and wonder at the magnitude of the enormous mess hall which was a general meeting-place and ballroom and the very heart of the inland business.

With the arrival of McTavish and the other merchants from Montreal, the season's business really commenced. Each day new brigades brought in other wintering partners and the bales of pelts for which Grand Portage existed. Now the log shacks flanking the main building were filled with clerks and interpreters who worked from dawn to dusk in the stores and workshops, the counting-house and even the stone magazine. As each brigade of Montreal canoes arrived, throngs of pork-eaters surged into the stockade, eager for the feed of bread and pork, butter and an extra tot of rum which every man received at the journey's end. After six weeks of living on cornmeal mush, bread and pork was a welcome change. But the northmen rushed for the feast as they arrived at the end of their long journey. They hadn't tasted a bite of bread since leaving Grand Portage a year or more before. They were starved for a change from their monotonous diet of pemmican and fish. And they were equally starved for news. Even when they had eaten all they could eat and received messages from their families and friends, they didn't want to leave the post to return to their tents. They had to shake hands again, and again. Some of them boasted so much about their experiences of the past year, the hardships and dangers they had survived, that fights flared up. A few, unable to settle down, cooled off in the lock-up, for the business had to go on, and the season was short.

Fortunately most had cooled off by the time the highlight of the annual meeting's social life was announced, the ball. That was an event no one could bear to miss.

As dusk fell at the end of the long summer day, Indian camp fires twinkled along the shore, sending rippling reflections across the bay. Beside their upside-down canoes the pork-eaters cooked their suppers early. Across the little dividing creek dozens of northmen's camp fires cast dancing shadows on crooked rows of weathered tents. Everyone was busy preparing for the big event.

Inside the stockade watches were posted along the gallery to guard against fire, one of the constant dangers in this settlement built entirely of timber. In the great hall itself hundreds of candles in great candelabra cast a festive light on the merchants and *bourgeois*, clerks and interpreters who had already dined on quantities of beef, salt pork, ham, fish, venison, Indian corn, bread and butter, tea and wine and spirits. Surfeited with the food and drink brought up to the depot at great expense, they had all toasted "the Mother of All the Saints". The pipers were tuning their pipes, the fiddlers plucking strings.

For this highlight of the year everyone dressed in his—or her—best. The gentlemen sported their fine fawn or grey coats and breeches and gay silk vests. Every pork-eater appeared in a clean shirt and with his brightest hand-woven sash about his waist; northmen in new buckskin short shirts and leggings. Indian chiefs wore their medals and blankets, braves had daubed their faces and chests, girls donned their finest beaded white-buckskin tunics. Soon the great mess hall was filled. Everyone jostled everyone else. And then, as the bagpipe and fiddles broke into the first lilting tune the jostling stopped as if by magic. The old folks squatted along the walls amid black-eyed babies propped up in board cradles. Pork-eaters and northmen pranced to the centre of the room. They and their partners awaited the customary signal for the ball to open.

That year it was Simon McTavish who stood up among the gentlemen to lead the opening reel. A buzz of excitement spread across the room. Which maiden would the *bourgeois* choose? Who, indeed, but the comeliest. McTavish nodded to a chief's daughter. Proud and smiling she took her place beside him. The fiddler nodded to the piper. Each gentleman squired a pretty girl. Soon everyone who could, danced reels and squares till the floor was filled with prancing feet. The piper played faster, fiddlers tapped their toes quicker with every familiar tune. Occasionally a fight broke out, soon settled, if a couple of pork-eaters wanted to dance with the same girl. Only when a northman and a pork-eater coveted the same girl was the fight serious enough to command the firm hand of the *bourgeois*.

Late in the evening everyone paused for food—great platters of cold venison, pork and fish, great piles of bread, and gallons of scalding hot tea. And then the dance continued till dawn brightened the lead-coloured surface of Lake Superior.

Next day the business continued, a little slower, perhaps, but without serious interruption. At the usual hour the *bourgeois* and clerks were at their desks and counters, or checking trade goods and pelts in the warehouses. They could afford to lose no time in sending the northmen back to the interior, if the northmen were to reach their distant posts before freeze-up.

Planning the next season's trade was a serious business for the proprietors. But it was equally as momentous for young clerks and northmen on their first trip beyond Grand Portage.

No man concerned failed to be at the mess hall on placement day. By that time *bourgeois* and clerks had assigned each man to the district where trade would be carried on. Where would each man winter? That was the great question. Would it be far up the Saskatchewan River? On the wide prairies where pemmican would be traded with Blackfoot and Plains Cree Indians? On the Athabasca River, recently reached by that sturdy trader, Peter Pond? In the low muskrat country about Cumberland House where Samuel Hearne had built the Hudson's Bay Company's first challenging depot short of Hudson Bay?

Sometimes a young man's heart dropped when he learned where he was to go. For it was one thing to dream of adventure in the fur trade while you were with hundreds of other men at Grand Portage. It was entirely different to discover that you might be spending two or even three years practically alone in a remote area. Then many a young newcomer like William McGillivray longed to be back in Scotland or Montreal or Albany. But there could be no turning back. Soon each northman would be heading west, up and over the nine-mile Grand Portage itself.

The height of land between Lake Superior and the Lake-of-the-Woods country runs close to the west shore of Lake Superior. It gives the area its magnificent scenery. Rising in many places to a thousand feet above this lake, it was a formidable obstacle to canoe travel.

The Indians, with small canoes, used to carry both craft and packs up the back-breaking portage to the upper Pigeon River, named for the swarms of carrier pigeons that darkened the sky over the region. Pigeon River drops in a series of spectacular falls to Lake Superior, but above the falls it is passable for canoes. Up there, where the carrying-place joined the river, the northwest fur trade established Fort Charlotte, a dreary cluster of fly-infested log shacks named in honour of George III's queen.

For a month during the hottest days of summer a stream of men trudged between Grand Portage and Fort Charlotte, in another of the fur trade's essential shuttles. Pork-eaters carried cargoes between the two posts as part of their contract, as did some northmen. In hot, dry weather or through greasy stretches of ankle-deep mud every man carried two or more ninety-pound packs on each trip. For each pack carried beyond the eight stipulated in his contract, he received an extra Spanish dollar, and dollars were coveted. Looking like apes, their arms swinging free, bent under the packs piled on their backs and secured by the broad band of the tumpline across the forehead, they shuttled up and down, carrying supplies for the northwest one way, pelts from the northwest the other. To relieve the monotony of the gruelling trips, each man tried to outdo the others in taunting them about their slowness or their clumsiness or the fact that they carried only two packs. And in a mixture of French and Indian every man cursed endlessly and impartially friends who had wooed the girl he wanted, and the blistering blights of blackflies and mosquitoes.

Over the years those French-Canadian canoemen and their forebears had developed regular stopping-places along the nine-mile carrying-place, known as *poses*. Sixteen *poses* marked Grand Portage, varying in length from six to eight hundred yards. Each originally was more than a resting-place. In the early days it was a temporary depot. To prevent possible theft, every pack and keg was brought up to the first *pose* before any were carried to the next.

As the stream of goods and pelts flowed over the portage, the proprietors down in the mess hall grappled with their business problems. Grand Portage was a depot for the long-established southwest trade, as well as that of the newer northwest. Indeed, in 1779 when the North West Company was started, the southwest trade was twice as large as that of the northwest, and regarded as being the most valuable on the continent. Among partners in the North West Company some, like the McGills, had interest in both areas. After a few years, these men realized that it was impractical to manage business in such widespread territory. The original partners, all friends and neighbours in Montreal, decided to divide the trade.

As casually as though they were dealing a pack of cards, they portioned among themselves the known parts of the continent beyond Lake Superior through a sort of gentlemen's agreement. The McGills and their associates would do business in the southwest; Simon McTavish and his partners would take the northwest.

James McGill doubtless thought he had done a fine stroke of business in getting the southwest trade. But McTavish and the Frobishers had judged that the American Revolution, just over, would ruin the fur trade of the Upper Mississippi through inroads of settlers. They knew, too, that the beaver in the southwest didn't compare in quality and quantity with northern beaver, and Peter Pond had recently discovered new beaver meadows on the Athabasca River. Indeed, from Pond's accounts there seemed no end to the rivers to be exploited.

William McGillivray felt that excitement flash through him again as he listened while his uncle and the other partners of the North West Company drew up a new agreement in 1784. Now the Nor'Westers were confident they would enjoy an actual monopoly of the trade beyond Lake Superior. Of course there was the Hudson's Bay Company, but the old chartered English company was still doing most of its business along Hudson Bay. The only real opposition, if any, would come from the Detroit firm headed by John Gregory whose traders had already run foul of Peter Pond in the Athabasca country. Gregory had a clerk, a young Scot named Alexander Mackenzie, who might develop into a real rival if he ever became a partner of the Detroit firm. Simon McTavish and his fellow Nor'Westers kept an alert eye on likely opponents. That way they knew whom to crush. They also knew how to do it.

"Je Suis un Homme du Nord!"

A few days out of Fort Charlotte—it depended on weather and the size of the brigade—the northwest route crossed the *Hauteur de Terre*, the Height of Land. This was more than a ridge where all the streams behind the west-bound brigade flowed to the Great Lakes and all those ahead to the vague, remote north. For the streams flowing into Lake Superior also flowed homeward for each white man in the early fur trade. At the Height of Land each newcomer might feel an overwhelming panic, part homesickness and part excitement. But no matter what he felt, he soon learned to keep his feelings to himself.

Perhaps it was because the Height of Land was more than geography that a ceremony marked each man's first crossing, a ceremony similar to that performed on ships crossing the equator.

From the moment each new-comer left Grand Portage he heard about the initiation ceremony. Indeed, he had likely heard about it from old hands back in his mother's kitchen at home. By the time the moment arrived he felt like a young Indian about to face the fearful rites of manhood.

Beside the first north-flowing stream the entire well-regulated, disciplined brigade came to a halt. Everyone gathered about him—canoemen, guides and interpreters, clerks and the *bourgeois* if one were present. The oldest guide presided—perhaps a man of thirty who had made more trips to the *pays d'en haut* than any other man present. It mattered not that the new-comer was Simon McTavish's nephew. Scot or Frenchman, clerk or *voyageur* or wintering partner, the ceremony must be performed, and in French, the language of the fur trade. So William

McGillivray stood, one hot late summer's day, where the streams flowed in two directions. He had taken off his hat, and a tingling sensation pricked the back of his neck. Encircling him stood the men who had become his companions. The oldest guide had already taken out his knife. Testing its blade on his thumb, the guide looked carefully into the woods. Satisfied at last, he stepped to a cedar beside the path. With a firm swipe he cut off a sturdy bough, and dipped it into the near-by stream.

"Kneel!"

McGillivray dropped to his knees, amid the now silent company, and bent his head. Soon the oldest guide had thoroughly drenched him with the wet cedar bough. Then he made the two-fold promise, repeating the words after the guide. He promised, on his honour, never to permit another new-comer to pass over the Height of Land without a similar ceremony. And he swore never to kiss a *voyageur*'s wife without her consent. Everyone cheered. A quick burst of shot broke on the air. The fusillade was fired quickly because no one could wait another minute to drink a toast to the newest northman.

The toast was the real reason for the ceremony, everyone said. But the *voyageurs* knew there was more to it. Only a few hundred men made the long, dangerous trip west from Montreal or Grand Portage each year. And back in the little houses along the St. Lawrence or Ottawa rivers every boy listened raptly when a northman told tales of wintering in the Indian country.

"Je suis un homme du nord!"

It was a proud, swaggering boast. Everyone hearing it knew that it meant rigorous portages and long journeys, visits to strange lands and perilous encounters with storms and wild animals and other countless dangers of that fierce and rugged country.

Beyond Rainy River, "the most beautiful river in the north" according to the fur-traders, the North West Company established a post at Rainy Lake—*Lac La Pluie*. Rainy Lake post was used partly as a depot for collecting great quantities of wild rice, harvested by the Indians in the area's maze of streams by flailing the kernels with paddles into slow-moving canoes. It was also an advance depot for the Athabascan crews.

To make better time and because of the tortuous nature of many of the streams, small canoes were used beyond Grand Portage. Each was roughly half the size of the great Montreal canoes. Lighter, also, than the Montreal canoes which weighed five hundred pounds, northern canoes weighed only three hundred pounds and could be carried, usually right side up, over portages, by the steersman and bowman. Each northern canoe held twenty-five ninety-pound packs instead of the sixty loaded into Montreal canoes, and was manned by four or five *voyageurs*. Even fewer packs were carried in the Athabasca canoes, so as to make better time on the four-thousand-mile Rainy Lake–Fort Chipewyan round trip between spring thaw and autumn freeze-up.

Beyond the Lake of the Woods lay the worst white water on the long trip. The Winnipeg River was dangerous all the way to Lake Winnipeg. But worst of all was the stretch known as the *Rivière Blanche*. Here cataract after cataract of boiling torrent necessitated many carryings. Year after year *voyageurs* drowned even on the short stretches considered safe for canoes. Yet most remained scornful of the dangers involved. Most could tell first-hand experiences similar to that described by William

McGillivray's brother, Duncan, about the second of seven portages within sight of each other.

"One of the canoes imprudently advanced too near the Fall to unload . . . After the goods were debarked, the upper end through some negligence was suddenly carried out by the current with the steersman suspended after it, and the foreman attempting to retain his end was also carried away . . . They were hurled down through three successive cascades, the canoe several times overwhelmed with water and threatened every moment with being dashed to pieces on the rocks. After arriving at the dreadful whirlpool it remained a considerable time under water. At length the current drove it to shore, with the men still hanging on. Tho' they at first seemed insensible, after a little assistance they recovered and before night renewed their labours as if nothing had happened to them."

The wild water of the Winnipeg River flowed into shallow, long Lake Winnipeg. No carrying-places here, no dangerous rapids. Winds often whipped the shallow water to waves that seemed mountainous from a low-lying canoe. But who cared about winds or waves? Lake Winnipeg was the great race course of the entire cross-continent canoe route.

Usually the Athabascan brigades started those races. Meeting other North West Company brigades or occasionally a free-trader's canoes at Bas de la Rivière near the lake's entrance, the Athabascans boasted that they could out-paddle any crew on Lake Winnipeg. Perhaps a little drunk from an extra tot of rum after the heart-breaking passage of the Winnipeg River, the others took them on—brigades destined for the Saskatchewan or Swan rivers. Usually the race was unfair from the beginning, because of the lighter loading of the Athabascans, and because those crews had been carefully chosen to stand the rigours of that annual four-thousand-mile return trip down from Fort Chipewyan to Rainy Lake and back.

As many as a hundred canoes raced together, each brigade keeping in formation. A good *voyageur* paddled forty strokes to the minute, and could keep up that pace from dawn to dusk with brief stops for breakfast and nooning and an occasional smoke when the guide called one. Forty strokes to the minute was considered a good, safe pace by the proprietors. But the men liked speed. They needed a change of excitement after risking their lives—and the company's cargo—on white water. Across grey, choppy Lake Winnipeg the Athabascans hurled their taunts The others increased their speed. Forty-five strokes to the minute. Fifty strokes. The lake was wide. The excitement mounted. If one of the heavier-laden Saskatchewan or Swan Lake canoes slackened, the other crew taunted.

"So you want to stop, eh—old men! Old like a tortoise!"

Fifty-five paddle strokes to the minute. The rival northmen were like wrestlers with their reputations at stake. No time now for smokes. No time for songs. Guides, caught up in the excitement, hacked off hunks of pemmican which the straining *voyageurs* chewed as they paddled faster, faster till they verged on exhaustion. And as exhaustion increased, judgment waned. Sixty strokes to the minute. Occasionally a man fell overboard while the canoes sped on.

On one occasion two brigades actually paddled for forty hours before a *bourgeois* ordered the men to cease. Generally there was little rancour after the canoes were beached on the low shore, though a space separated the camp sites as insurance against fights. The *bourgeois* opened a keg of rum. After a tot and supper of boiled pemmican and wild rice, everyone slept. For years to come that forty-hour endurance test was something to talk about from Montreal to Fort Chipewyan—and beyond.

Next day there would be the three-mile portage at Grand Rapids at the mouth of the Saskatchewan River. And then more stretches of open water on the Lower Saskatchewan where a sail could be hoisted. Now some of the *voyageurs* were nearing their winter's destination. And whether at one of the prairie posts, at Cumberland House on the Saskatchewan, at Ile à la Crosse on the Churchill, or distant Fort Chipewyan on Lake Athabasca, each home-coming was the same. Only the degree of home-coming excitement increased with the distance. Below the last river bend before the post, a stop to shave and clean up—the northmen did as pork-eaters did on nearing Grand Portage. And then back into the canoes, back to the cramped positions and the gay songs beloved of the *voyageur*. There were many *chansons* popular for that last swinging paddle toward the post. None was more beloved than "Lisette": "Who has no love, has no happy days".

La belle Lisette
Chantait l'autre jour.
La belle Lisette
Chantait l'autre jour.

Les échos répètent
"Qui n'a pas d'amour
Qui n'a pas d'amour
N'a pas de beaux jours".

It was a hard life. But then, as every *voyageur* knew, it wasn't supposed to be easy. For excitement there was the trip to Grand Portage and the races on Lake Winnipeg. And the winter's trapping and trading wasn't all boredom. Maybe a man would travel with *M'sieu* Pond who asked so many questions about the natives and the streams the natives travelled. Or it might be *M'sieu* Joseph Frobisher, a good and kindly *bourgeois*, generous with the rum when it brought many good pelts. One might even enjoy swaggering before those simple servants of the Hudson's Bay Company who had no rum and who must be so careful with their meagre supplies of trade goods, tobacco and brandy. Indeed, the *voyageurs* made fun of "the English"—when they met them along the rivers—taunting them about the cautious trading methods imposed by their employers in London. The English, they charged scornfully, were as unenterprising as their masters, waiting a hundred years on the shores of Hudson Bay for the natives to go to them with their pelts. But they, the Nor'Westers, had plenty of rum, plenty of tobacco, and they did not have to be miserly with beads and blankets. They were the finest canoemen in the world, who could travel anywhere. Of course they would get the finest pelts.

They were proud, those *voyageurs*, as they had cause to be. They were confident that they, and their North West Company *bourgeois*, could easily outwit the free-traders from Detroit, including the enterprising Alexander Mackenzie. They knew that the Montreal fur trade depended on them. It was this knowledge, in later years, that led every *voyageur* to aspire to paddling an express canoe. Paddling an express canoe was the highest honour for a canoeman. With four or five picked men he would rush the mail or a *bourgeois* at twice the usual speed. The record set by those men who boasted: "*Je suis un homme du nord*" was made by six northmen who paddled Roderick McKenzie, in a light canoe, from Rainy Lake to Fort Chipewyan in a month and four days. The distance is two thousand miles.

The Struggle Begins

Simon McTavish was sure of one thing: to prosper, the North West Company must have a monopoly of the fur trade of the vast interior. Fort Chipewyan, on Lake Athabasca, was a good three thousand miles from Montreal. Everything needed in the trade, except food which the Nor'Westers bartered from Indians beyond Grand Portage, had to be carried all that distance. If the company was to survive, it must keep costs low enough to show a profit. The Nor'Westers could be slow and careful, like the Hudson's Bay Company—or they could use dash and enterprise. The latter was the only course for McTavish.

From the beginning McTavish had favoured Highland Scots. They were of his own blood, and he knew many of their families. But he also knew that Highlanders were hardy men accustomed to a stern life among their native hills and glens. They were men who had learned to make the most of what was offered and to do it without grumbling. They were good fighters, too, and that counted. They were afraid of nothing in the world except failure. Within a few years of the signing of the first North West Company agreement, its list of employees read like a list of the clans of Scotland.

They were a fine combination, those young Highlanders and their spirited French-Canadian *voyageurs*. McTavish apprenticed all three of his nephews, William, Duncan and Simon McGillivray, to the fur trade. Each knew, as a good Nor'Wester must know almost by instinct, when their toiling canoemen needed an extra tot of rum to paddle to a post by nightfall. Like

Alexander Henry's nephew, Alexander Henry the Younger, they had a sense of the sweep of the business. They understood the conditions under which the trade existed: a man must be ruthless at times to survive. Yet most of the Highlanders were friendly, if given their own way. They could be generous as well as ruthless.

But the Nor'Westers weren't the only fur-traders who were brave and ruthless and generous, and who saw the supreme advantages of monopoly. Others coveted the riches of the interior. Most weren't strong enough or sufficiently well organized to put up any serious opposition. Only the Detroit firm—now Gregory, McLeod & Company—merited the respect of rivals in the opinion of the Nor'Westers.

All along this group had stubbornly refused to join the North West Company. It, too, had attracted many of those proud, fighting Highlanders and the best French-Canadian *voyageurs* it could engage. Alexander Mackenzie and his cousin, Roderick, had become wintering partners of the Detroit firm along with two traders of long experience, Peter Pangman and John Ross, and a Swiss trader named Waden. At last the two companies met in the rich Athabasca country.

Both companies had given their employees similar instructions. Those instructions were brief and simple: get the pelts! But the Detroiters hadn't reckoned on Peter Pond.

Peter Pond had been the first white man to cross Methye Portage, the height of land separating the drainage system of Hudson Bay from that of the Arctic. "Old Peter Pond" the younger men called him, because he had been one of the first little group of traders to reach the northwest in 1775. Pond had traded pemmican with the Blackfoot and Plains Cree Indians on the prairies to supply his men in the remote Athabasca country. He had persuaded the natives to trap, and persuaded his own men to paddle and portage kegs of rum and bales of trade goods over all the rough water and carrying-places from Montreal, three thousand miles away. He had snow-shoed up and down the frozen streams in winter. He naturally regarded the Athabasca and the Upper Churchill River territory as his by right of discovery. That country belonged to the North West Company.

Pond had even drawn a map of the country, the first ever made of the northwest. He had asked the natives about streams and carrying-places, and given them rum and trinkets when they drew rough sketches for him on birch bark or smooth sand beaches. And during long, bitter cold winter evenings he had thawed out his frozen ink and laboriously worked at that map while his partners and clerks yarned among themselves or feasted with the natives. He had worked, too, handicapped by lack of education and in spite of smiles when he talked about finding a land route to the Pacific.

And then one morning while he was at Lac La Ronge his men told him that another trader had arrived, and was already building a log house, a man named Etienne Waden, of Gregory, McLeod & Company. A free-trader!

Hudson's Bay Company people had traded along the upper Churchill River near Lac La Ronge, but Pond had put up with them. The Detroiter was another sort of challenge entirely. Yet Pond was glad of the company of any white man in the lonely, remote wilderness. He tried to get along with Waden, and the two men made a casual agreement to pool their trade goods and share their supplies. But Pond couldn't hide his resentment entirely. A quarrel developed in February, and was patched up. A few weeks later Waden and Pond clashed again. Tempers flared. Either Pond or one of his men fired a shot, hitting Waden, who died shortly after. Later Pond was tried for murder at Montreal, and acquitted.

Some of the newer, younger Nor'Westers got along with opponents from the Gregory, McLeod Company; William McGillivray and Roderick McKenzie wintered and traded near each other at Ile à la Crosse, and enjoyed each other's company. Even Pond might have lived amicably near McKenzie, but he couldn't put up with John Ross, who later headed the Gregory, McLeod firm near Fort Chipewyan.

That winter Ross built a couple of log houses in sight of Chipewyan, and erected a strong stockade about them. Ross had been left out of partnership in the original North West Company, and from the first took out his grudge on Pond. Pond was getting old in the fur trade. He had suffered years of hardship and the frustration of trying to draw his maps without enough formal education. And here was Ross with plenty of rum and trade goods, forcing Pond to go out after the natives with more rum than Pond felt he could afford for their pelts. And in the country he had discovered and explored, the country where he had worked up trade! In a scuffle with two of Pond's men, Ross was shot and killed. For the second time Pond was tried for murder and acquitted, but suspicion lingered.

When William McGillivray and McKenzie arrived at Grand Portage the summer following the shooting with word of Ross's death, both companies became alarmed. Already there were rumours from England that the British Government was considering action against the fur-traders if violent competition continued. As a result McTavish was able to convince the Detroiters, especially Alexander Mackenzie, that the opposition was dangerous to both interests. That summer—1787—a new North West Company agreement was drawn up. It absorbed the only strong Nor'Wester opposition from the east.

The summer meeting of 1787 was a triumph for Simon McTavish. The new agreement divided the company into twenty shares, so as to make provision for the former partners of Gregory, McLeod & Co. But this year, amid the gaiety and feasting usual during the brief summer meeting, there was a feeling of achievement. Not only were they now sure of the all important food supply from the prairies, but the trade in pelts could go on smoothly. One of the outstanding features of the new agreement provided that shares could not be sold outside the organization. They would be reserved as a reward for experienced clerks, including McTavish's nephews. This in itself strengthened the already strong *esprit de corps* throughout the company. Now with the addition of men such as Alexander Mackenzie and his cousin Roderick—instead of the opposition—they were a truly great company.

In the meantime Benjamin Frobisher had died in Montreal. McTavish had taken the opportunity to suggest to Joseph Frobisher that they form a company to supply the Nor'Westers. McTavish, Frobisher Company soon acquired controlling stock in the North West Company, with provision that they should handle all the Nor'Westers' Montreal business. They set up a fur sales depot in London. Acting as agents, and with adequate capital, they were in a position to buy corn for the pork-eaters at the lowest prices, and trade goods well in advance, so that both could be on hand at the various depots and trading-posts as needed.

The North West Company partners were now, more than ever before, leading citizens in the growing Canadian colony. Indeed some had already retired with fortunes. The McGills had become wealthy Montreal merchants. Others had bought seigniories in Quebec Province or estates in Scotland. Each year the profits of the company built new mansions in Montreal, and Joseph Frobisher's Beaver Hall became a centre of social life famed for its lavish hospitality. The business and politics of Canada was largely in the hands of Nor'Westers.

But Simon McTavish knew that he hadn't yet really achieved a monopoly of the northwestern fur trade. He had united the Montreal and Detroit interests. There was still the Hudson's Bay Company.

So far McTavish had paid little heed to the old English company. Cumberland House, built by Samuel Hearne on the Lower Saskatchewan in 1774, was strategically located on the main route for all canoes travelling to the real northwest. But Cumberland House had merely reminded the Nor'Westers that there was an English company claiming a monopoly. The English company supplied so little rum and trade goods that at times the Nor'Westers had generously shared tobacco and food with Hearne. They had travelled and traded, pushing farther on each year as they explored new streams, much as the French had done before them. When they met the Hudson's Bay Company's

Orkney servants, they had either laughed at or pitied them for the clumsy fellows they were with a canoe. And, as McTavish knew, the English company had paid no dividends to its shareholders for several years, though that was partly due to the epidemic of smallpox which had killed so many Indians. But, after having paid a steady 10 per cent dividend for years, the Hudson's Bay Company was now paying none.

McTavish was too shrewd a man not to know that something different was happening at last. Wintering partners coming down to Grand Portage reported new Hudson's Bay Company trading-posts up the Saskatchewan in the Upper Churchill River country, and out on the prairies where pemmican was traded. The Orkneymen were trying to learn how to handle a canoe, and already their progress was noticeable. There was a rumour that the Hudson's Bay Company had engaged a French-Canadian free trader to teach its factors how to pack their trade goods to fit into canoes. None of these counted much in itself. Together they suggested that the English company was at last trying to compete seriously with the Nor'Westers for beaver and other pelts. And if they ever did manage their inland trade to match the Nor'Westers' prices, their much shorter haul by way of Hudson Bay could become a real menace. Indeed, the shorter haul by way of Hudson Bay became more menacing with each new territory the Nor'Westers opened, because each new territory lengthened the Montreal trade route and added to its cost.

Simon McTavish surveyed the North West Company empire, stretching from Montreal to the Athabasca River, and even north of Lake Superior to include the Lakes Nipigon and

Temiskaming territory, close to Hudson Bay. The colony of Canada still depended on the fur trade to keep ships coming into and sailing out of Montreal harbour, and McTavish was determined to keep the harbour busy. So he boarded one of those ships late in November 1790 and sailed for London.

In London William Pitt was then Prime Minister of England. Simon McTavish went to see him about the Montreal fur trade which not only meant everything to the colony, but which contributed so much business to England herself. He asked Mr. Pitt to abolish the Hudson's Bay Company monopoly. The Prime Minister replied that nothing short of an Act of Parliament could abolish the monopoly, a most unlikely feat in view of the great influence of the company's individual shareholders in London. McTavish then went to the Hudson's Bay Company itself with an offer to lease transit rights through its Hudson Bay ports. That, the Hudson's Bay Company refused. For the Nor'Westers there was now no alternative but to continue the all-out trade war, a situation much to McTavish's taste.

Au Façon du Nord

*S*trange music entertained the Nor'Wester. There were the songs he sang as he paddled, *chansons* already old in France before the *voyageur* adapted them to the rhythm of the paddle. There were tunes played on bagpipe and fiddle on the rare festive occasions such as a brigade's home-coming. Sometimes he heard sighing music in the trees on long, lonely trips. He may even have regarded as music the fights that flared between men quick to use their fists, men whose tempers were often stretched to bowstring tension through prolonged hardship. But no music in the trade was sweeter than the steady drumming *lub-dub, lub-dub, lub-dub* of Indian women pounding dried buffalo meat.

To a fur-trader that was music with a meaning. It was prairie music and music of the parkland along the South Saskatchewan, the Red and the Assiniboine rivers. It was a motif of survival and discovery and success. No one put it down on paper as music, perhaps because it was felt and remembered rather than heard.

At the thought of it a picture sprang to a fur-trader's mind— a picture of a group of Indian women pounding steadily, rhythmically all day long. Some were old and unlovely, others were young and pretty. Old or young, plain or pretty, most made pemmican. On the prairie they squatted round a huge buffalo robe spread out on the short grass; in the parkland at the edge of the prairie where a few great trees survived centuries of bush fires, they pounded pemmican in a hollow log. The hollow log sound carried clear and far on the air. But by laying an ear against the ground, a man could hear the thumping on a buffalo hide, like a muffled drum, for miles. It was like a heartbeat.

The pemmican pounding began soon after the hunters had finished the buffalo hunt. Scarcely had the men ridden into camp to tell of the number of great bulls or fat cows they had killed when the women started to dress the game. That was old women's work, or reserved for slaves. Younger women cut the succulent flesh into strips which they dried on racks over willow fires or in the sun. By either method, the hunger-exciting smell of drying meat lingered in every fur-trader's mind as part of the music. It was as unforgettable as the weird chants that accompanied the rhythmic rise and fall of wooden-handled stone mallets on hide or hollow log. For pemmican was essential to the fur trade. Without it the northwestern third of the continent would have had an entirely different story of discovery.

For decades there was no other food available in the vast interior except a little wild rice, or fish or game when the hunting was good. On his first day out from Grand Portage Nor'Wester Daniel Harmon wrote in his journal what every man eventually experienced: "I have this day, for the first time in my life, eaten no bread or biscuit". Like other new-comers Harmon didn't realize then that he would eat no bread until his return to Grand Portage.

On long canoe trips where highly concentrated, highly nourishing food was essential, pemmican was ideal. Packaged in ninety-pound lots in buffalo-hide bags, it was made from that dried, pounded buffalo meat—fifty pounds of lean meat with forty pounds of melted fat poured on top to seal it. In quality it varied with the women who made it. Some of the women were careful and very clean. They seasoned their product with fresh or dried saskatoon berries. They took great care blending the fat, using equal parts from the entrails of the buffalo and the sweet, tasty *dépouilles*, the two strips that lay along the animal's backbone. Carefully blended fat ensured pemmican that didn't easily get rancid. But not all the women were careful. Bits of twigs and grass and pebbles, and even their own hair and that of the dogs common around every camp got into their pemmican, and the fat might be too soft to keep and not tastefully blended. No salt seasoned any pemmican, because salt would add to a *voyageur*'s thirst.

Good or bad, or average, there was seldom enough pemmican available to supply the fur trade as it increased toward the beginning of the nineteenth century. By that time the Nor'Westers had eight times as many men in the interior as the Hudson's Bay Company. To maintain their trade supremacy they imported vast quantities of beads and calico and rum to persuade the Indian women to make more and more pemmican. Late each summer clerks at the warehouses along the Red and Saskatchewan rivers piled the ninety-pound bags higher and higher till they reached the high-pitched roofs. But soon returning brigades of hungry *voyageurs* loaded their canoes and paddled off to the Upper Saskatchewan and the Athabasca and beyond, and the stocks dwindled. Some years there was not enough for the down trip in the spring. March never came without anxious eyes scanning the southern skies for the first wedges of geese which would save the precious pemmican for canoe rations.

There never was a more completely nourishing, easily transported single item of food. A hungry northern canoeman needed eight or ten pounds of fresh meat a day, and game was often scarce. He needed more fish, and night-set nets at times yielded none. But with a couple of pounds of pemmican a day, plus a tot of rum, he paddled cheerfully from dawn to sundown. He preferred it boiled over his supper fire. If the season was late, however, and ice threatened the streams he ate it as it came from the bag. He might even hack off a hunk with his knife, and chew as he paddled.

And so *voyageurs* and *bourgeois* alike knew how much the fur trade depended on Indian women for food; probably only the latter realized how large a part Indian women played in keeping the tall ships sailing in and out of Montreal harbour. *Voyageurs* knew, if they ever paused to think about it, how much they depended on Indian women to keep their bark canoes afloat. For it was they who carefully examined each over-turned canoe every time the brigade stopped, mending rents with watape prepared from cedar roots and sealing the mend with gum. Both the watape and the gum were gathered and prepared by women. Women netted the snow-shoes, too. They made every man's moccasins, and *voyageur* and *bourgeois* alike wore out several pairs a year. And because an Indian seldom carried a bundle for fear of losing face, traders depended on those hardworking women as porters when they lacked a horse—or a dogdrawn *travois*.

Most white men soon realized that Indian girls were attractive. Daniel Harmon, a strictly brought-up New Englander, boasted at Grand Portage on his way to the northwest that he certainly wouldn't marry a native. But when a chief offered him his daughter, a quiet, nicely behaved girl of fourteen, Harmon agreed to think about it. Since there were no priests or other clergy within a couple of thousand miles, the ceremony was performed after the manner of the country: Harmon gave the chief a present, together with a keg of dilute rum. He planned to leave his Indian wife with some other trader when he retired from the northwest. But when the time came, nineteen years later, he couldn't bear to leave her. He took her and their children back home with him.

Alexander Henry, the Younger, tried desperately—according to his journal—to free himself from an Indian girl whom he brought to his house following a New Year's party at one of the prairie posts. He went off buffalo-hunting. The girl was still at his house on his return. Henry told her she must go back to her tribe. But still she remained. "The devil couldn't have got rid of her," he said. Eventually she became his wife, also after the manner of the country, and they remained happily married until he was accidentally drowned several years later.

David Thompson, the great geographer who left the Hudson's Bay Company to join the Nor'Westers, married a Métis girl, Charlotte Small. And many other Nor'Westers had native wives. Usually there was a simple ceremony, *au façon du nord*—a gift to the girl's father; a horse, perhaps, or a blanket or gun, and small keg of dilute rum. On the whole these were successful marriages. The women were pleasant companions, and good home-makers under conditions which few white women would have endured. Gradually over the years their children grew up about the various posts, forming the first settlements in the northwest.

But the Nor'Westers discovered that a wife costs something,

one reason why the Hudson's Bay Company forbade such alliances. When there were hundreds of them—and, indeed, at least one Nor'Wester maintained two wives at two different posts at the company's expense—the cost became considerable. As the Montreal traders discovered new trapping areas and extended their supply lines, they were forced to consider their expenses. Most of the time they were too fully occupied with trading and exploring to trouble themselves over accounts. Were they not virtual rulers of half a continent? Should they not live like rulers?

At Grand Portage, during the summer meetings, Simon McTavish announced that this one item of expense must stop. Henceforth all Nor'Wester *bourgeois*, clerks, *voyageurs* and guides must support their own wives and families. The gentlemen concerned listened tolerantly. They had heard McTavish— "the marquis", as a few of his associates came to call him as he grew older—bring up this item year after year. A few applauded. Some merely smiled. Most forgot the ruling as soon as they were back at their inland posts.

Never having wintered in the Indian country, McTavish couldn't understand the customs from personal experience. But as head of a great company, he must frown alike on extravagant practices and questionable morals, for not every Nor'Wester regarded his Indian marriage as enduring. Yet "the marquis" knew, as the shrewdest and best-informed wintering partner knew, that one of the main reasons why the North West Company out-traded the Hudson's Bay Company was this close relationship with Indian tribes. For the Nor'Westers weren't servants of a remote company. Many were actual partners; others were clerks with hope of becoming partners. They traded in their own interests, and on their own initiative. Married to a chief's daughter, a Nor'Wester had a good chance of securing her tribe's trade. If there was trouble—and trouble often flared up in the presence of too much rum—few braves would attack their chief's son-in-law.

In the heyday of the North West Company, its success depended as much on women in buckskin and beads as it did upon the canoe. And even canoe travel depended on them, for gum—to waterproof bark seams—was as essential to canoe transportation as oil is to modern transportation.

7

Alexander Mackenzie

*T*he year 1787 had been momentous for Alexander Mackenzie. At twenty-three he became a wintering part- ner of the North West Company, spent his first season at Lake Athabasca, and met Peter Pond, his greatest tutor.

Pond was then forty-seven, an old man in the fur trade. Ever since he was sixteen he had travelled by canoe and portage, snow-shoe and dog team. Forever asking questions of every knowledgeable Indian he met; studying land and water con- tours; hunching forward eagerly in his canoe as his *voyageurs* paddled him round each new bend in each new stream, he had become familiar with most of the known waterways of the northwest; indeed, he had travelled practically all of the known water routes north of the Upper Mississippi and west of his Milford Haven, Connecticut, birthplace.

Pond knew the hardships of the fur trade—heat, blackflies, mosquitoes in summer; bitter cold and too close contact with unwashed men in winter. Many a time he had gone to bed hun- gry when the pemmican supply was rationed and game scarce. His own lack of formal education and his partners' strong pref- erence for trade rather than exploration had irritated him greatly. But he wouldn't have chosen any other career in the world.

Young Mackenzie had soon sensed the older man's fanatical devotion to exploration. A few months at Fort Chipewyan con- vinced him that Pond had a better grasp of the geography of North America than any man he had ever met. Only four years previous the old man had presented his rough sketch map to the Congress of the Confederate States at Washington, the first map ever drawn of Northwestern Canada.

While in Washington Pond had heard about Captain Cook and his voyages. Cook's account of a great river flowing into the Pacific Ocean had fired the fur-trader-explorer's hopes afresh. Now he was sure there must be an overland link between the Atlantic and Pacific Oceans, a real northwest passage. Returning by the long, circuitous streams linking Washington with Lake Athabasca, Pond's thoughts had been occupied with only one idea when he wasn't busy with trading: how to find that way to the Pacific.

Pond had welcomed Mackenzie warmly as an eager young man, intelligent enough to understand his dreams. The two spent many a long winter evening by the light of a candle or the open fire. Of course Pond had discoursed on the local features of the fur trade—that was their business. But there had been hours for talk about the project that beckoned. Surely there could be only a narrow stretch of land between Fort Chipewyan and the Pacific Ocean—and Cook's great river! If a man followed the stream leading out of Lake Athabasca . . .

In the spring of 1788 Pond and Mackenzie went down to Grand Portage for the annual meeting and to dispose of the winter's fur trade. That summer the partners were concerned over the possible effects of John Ross's death, and Pond had to go on down to Montreal to face the charge of murder of which he was later acquitted. Mackenzie was promoted to manage Fort Chipewyan, then the largest and most important department of the North West Company. After receiving his instructions and stopping at Fort Charlotte for supplies, the twenty-four-year-old trader returned to Chipewyan—and memories of those long discussions with Peter Pond.

But the fur trade came first. Many Indian tribes living near the headwaters of the Churchill River and Lake Athabasca had long traded pelts with the Hudson's Bay Company at York Factory. One of the Nor'Westers' main concerns was to intercept that trade. So Mackenzie sent out his scouts to invite the chiefs to come to Fort Chipewyan. There he treated them to drinks of dilute rum, gave them tobacco and made numerous long speeches. He reminded them that the round trip to Hudson Bay would take almost seven months, and that it was a very arduous trip. If they traded with the Nor'Westers they would save themselves the long trip, and receive more trade goods than the English gave them. The English, he reminded the natives, didn't even care enough for their trade to bring their goods to the interior.

Mackenzie was carrying on Pond's tradition. He managed the fur trade with one hand and made plans for exploration with the other. How else could a man finance exploration except through trade? He must even find a competent lieutenant to manage the post when he finally set out to see what lay beyond Lake Athabasca. Roderick McKenzie, his cousin, could be trusted, and soon Roderick was being coached in the post's business.

All that winter Mackenzie's mind was in a ferment of questions. Did the stream flowing out of Lake Athabasca actually lead to the Pacific Ocean, as Pond believed? Was it indeed the long-sought northwest passage? On June 3, 1789, he finally set out from Chipewyan to seek answers to these two major questions. He took with him five experienced *voyageurs* and two Indian women. The women would look after clothing and prepare food for the little party, and help with the carrying.

Mackenzie didn't know where he was going. Like every other white man pushing his way into the interior before there were maps—and Pond, of course, had been able to sketch only territory and streams which he actually knew—he relied on Indian information plus his own keen observation. Right at the beginning he noted that the Slave River flowed in two directions. When the water is high in the Peace River, it flows into Lake Athabasca. Normally, it carries the outflow of Lake Athabasca north to Great Slave Lake.

Even in June drift-ice blocked much of Great Slave Lake; each morning fresh, thin ice had to be broken so that its sharp edges wouldn't knife through the thin bark of the canoe. After nine days, Mackenzie had only crossed the lake. A week more passed in skirting its north shore. Finally they reached the outlet of the lake, and the beginning of the fabled river. Again Mackenzie questioned himself and his Indian guides. How long would they be in reaching its mouth, wherever it might be? How many moons? Since no one could tell him, he cached several bags of pemmican for the return trip. Was he finally on the last lap of the legendary northwest passage?

The great river flowed northwest, the first large stream he had travelled that didn't flow east. Its current ran heavy and strong for the first few days. Then its course changed where a river—today's Liard—flowed in from the west. Mackenzie stayed on the larger stream, but now to his dismay his canoe headed northward. To the west loomed the mass of the Rocky Mountains, snow-covered and shining in the hot June sun. After more days of northerly travel the river was swollen by a large stream from the east—the Great Bear—obviously not the main river. Like a tiny chip, the canoe sped between the great ram-parts. Finally, on July 10, five weeks after he had left Chipewyan, Mackenzie stepped on a low shore which must be the estuary of the great stream. He had reached tidewater.

But surely this ocean, at least four thousand miles from Montreal, couldn't be the Pacific. Great cakes of ice dotted the bitterly cold water. Though the explorer stayed awake through the first night, the sun didn't set, and the night was cold. His experienced *voyageurs* begged him to return before they were all frozen in for the winter and their food all eaten.

Mackenzie had scarcely assured them that the river wouldn't freeze up in July, when another terror drove them to threaten mutiny. That day Mackenzie had been exploring the channels separating a group of low-lying islands when several enormous creatures broke water near the tiny canoe—whales. Each was large enough to dash the craft to bits with its tail. Mackenzie named the nearest land Whale Island, while his well-trained canoemen paddled with nervous strokes back to their tiny camp. Now they wouldn't stay another day, they threatened. Doubtless shaken himself, Mackenzie broached one of the last kegs of rum. When the men were warmed, he persuaded them to stay just a little longer while he explored this vast low-lying delta. When, ten days after their arrival at the delta, the tide rose during the night and swamped their tents, he reluctantly gave the order to break camp. He hadn't found a way to the Pacific. Though this was probably the greatest river on the continent, he had only one name for it—River of Disappointment.

The trip upstream quickly became gruelling. The men had to track, putting their arms through strong leather harness to haul the canoe along stretches of rough, rocky shore. The journey which had been so fast and easy travelling downstream was back-breaking and slow and laborious all the way up to Chipewyan. And for Mackenzie every weary step while his men tracked, every mile as he sat in the canoe reminded him that there was no northwest passage north of Lake Athabasca.

Next summer he travelled again to Grand Portage, with the furs Roderick had traded, to attend the annual meeting and announce his discovery. When Peter Pond heard that the newly discovered, nine-hundred-mile-long river didn't flow to the Pacific, that his calculations had been so far from fact, he was so disappointed that he quit the fur trade, sold his share to William McGillivray for £800, and took employment with the United States Government. Mackenzie's other partners showed little enthusiasm. No great celebrations marked the extension of the North West Company's empire, largely because the extension was north instead of west. Disappointed himself over the lack of enthusiasm over the discovery of so great a river, even though it wasn't the one he sought, Mackenzie decided to take a holiday. But first he bought another share in the North West Company, that owned by George McBeath, now about to retire.

For of course he was coming back. There must be a way to the Pacific. Before making another attempt to find that way, he needed further mathematical training, and better instruments. He went to England for both, and that much-needed holiday.

While Mackenzie was in England the Hudson's Bay Company, roused by the Nor'Westers' spirited competition, had sent Philip Turnor to survey Lake Athabasca. This was territory beyond that drained by "rivers flowing into Hudson Bay" after the 1670 charter, and the Nor'Westers might have laid charges of trespass. Fortunately, they didn't keep the English out by force, for Turnor located the position of Fort Chipewyan. Nothing in the world could have meant more to Alexander Mackenzie. Turnor's survey showed that Chipewyan was not a mere fifty leagues from the Pacific, as both Pond and Mackenzie had assumed. It was nearer three hundred leagues distant.

That fact considerably altered Mackenzie's plans on his return to the northwest. But he had gained perspective with his holiday, he was better equipped with instruments and more advanced mathematical training. Again arranging the Nor'Westers' Athabascan fur trade, he left Roderick McKenzie in charge. This time he would probe the stream that flowed from the southwest to join the Slave River a short distance from Lake Athabasca, the Peace River.

Three hundred leagues! What obstacles lay between him and the Pacific? Were there indeed mountains snow-capped throughout the year? Would he find a stream which would bring him to those mountains, and a pass through them? Again Mackenzie asked himself question after question. Again Indians sketched maps for him on birch bark or on a stretch of sand beside the river. Finally, to have as long a season as possible for this great adventure, he wintered far up the Peace, building a log fort on a little point six miles above the confluence of the Smoky and the Peace rivers, in the valley that is a thousand feet deep. The valley's very breadth and depth symbolized the magnitude of the task ahead.

But again trade must come first. All winter, while making his plans, Mackenzie sent out scouts to visit Indian bands, feasted the chiefs, handed out trade goods on credit, took in pelts. Early in the spring, before the ice went out of the river, he pressed and baled the pelts, wrote careful accounts of the winter's trade, ordered canoes built or repaired. And then he sent six canoes downstream to Grand Portage, laden with the winter's trade and his reports, as well as personal messages. He hoped to return safely. If he met with disaster the North West Company's business would go on.

On May 8, 1793—a full month earlier than his start for the Arctic four years previous—he left the little base at the confluence of the Smoky and Peace rivers and headed upstream. With him he had seven *voyageurs*—two had been with him on the Arctic trip—and two Indian hunters and interpreters. He had no guide, because none could be found who knew all the country between the Peace River and the Pacific. Truly, he must find his way as he went along.

The canoe was a large one for the northwest—twenty-five feet long with a four-foot-nine-inch beam. It was the lightest that would carry ten men, their food, arms, presents and Mackenzie's valuable instruments—in all three thousand pounds—and be carried by two men. As the canoe put into the stream, Mackenzie's two assistants left in charge of the post knelt to say special prayers for his safe return. They had already said a solemn farewell.

By the end of May, Mackenzie had reached the forks of the Peace. One rapid, churning through walls of soft rock, had all but wrecked the frail craft. Mackenzie had had to persuade his *voyageurs* to cut steps up the steep rock walls, and to haul their packs and the canoe up them to get out of the canyon. Again, as on the Arctic trip, they had begged him to go back. "Not yet," Mackenzie had replied, and each morning sent out scouts to explore the seemingly impassable country. At times, not knowing which way to go, they had climbed to the highest trees to get a glimpse of the mountainous country. But at the end of a week the trip continued.

At the forks Mackenzie faced a major decision. Should he follow the Parsnip or the Finlay? Travel due west or southwest? He decided on the latter. There were many such heart-breaking decisions to be faced before he even reached the Great Divide. Every mile of the way was tortuous and the Indians they met refused to guide the party; some said they thought white men knew everything and so would need no help from them. Often when the wrong stream had been followed, the route had to be re-traced. The high altitude near the Great Divide made the weather bitterly cold at night. Much of the precious shot was lost when the canoe capsized on a devil's cauldron of white water. By the end of June the men were thoroughly discouraged and exhausted. Without Mackenzie's superb, stubborn leadership and the warmth of the tiny issues of rum they would have mutinied a dozen times.

But over that Great Divide the streams flowed west. At last they were on the Pacific slope! Somewhere ahead lay the Pacific Ocean. Meticulously sharing every hardship with his men, eating exactly the same scant rations, for they met little game in the mountains, he persuaded them to go on—and on foot for the last part of the trip. After weeks of agonizing travel he knew they were nearing sea level. The tang of salt sea air told them the heart-breaking journey was almost ended. At last, as all the world now knows, Mackenzie and his little party stood on the sloping rock of Cape Menzies with the breadth of the Pacific Ocean before them—and the breadth of the North American continent behind. Using grease and vermilion, he wrote his famous inscription on the rock: "Alexander Mackenzie, from Canada, by land, the twenty-second of July, one thousand seven hundred and ninety-three."

He was the first white man to cross the continent north of the Spanish-held possessions, the first white man to cross overland from Montreal. There should have been a great burst of musket fire by way of celebration. There should have been an enormous feast. But Mackenzie had no shot or food to spare. Indeed, both were ominously low. The tribes they met near the coast were also ominously hostile. Mackenzie's men were terrified of being caught for the winter in those fearful mountain passes, cold even in July. Gaunt from gruelling travel and short rations, Mackenzie took a long look at this goal of a thousand explorers before him—and turned his back on it. At least he now knew that the Pacific Ocean could be reached overland by the route he would follow back to Chipewyan, back to Grand Portage and Montreal.

In four years he had travelled by canoe some ten thousand miles. He had extended the North West Company's empire a thousand miles farther north from Montreal, five hundred miles west. And he was bone weary of exhausting travel, of struggle with *voyageurs* whose fears he understood so well, of near starvation. He had made his last trip of exploration. Now he would spend a few years as an agent of the company, making regular trips in comparative luxury between Montreal and Grand Portage.

But after such long and exciting journeys he soon found the duties of an agent too monotonous for his restless energies. Knowing better than any man the cost and difficulties of pursuing the fur trade on the Pacific slope from overland, and the cost of the long haul from Montreal, he went to Niagara to consult Governor Simcoe of Upper Canada. With Simcoe he discussed plans for carrying on the Pacific trade by sea. He went to England to visit Lord Hobart, then Colonial Secretary, about a plan for uniting all the great chartered companies of British origin, such as the East India and Hudson's Bay companies. But always he found that his vision was too advanced for conservative business men of his day.

Back at Grand Portage, after his trip to England, his comparative youth and wide experience attracted a group of younger North West Company partners who felt they weren't getting the promotion they deserved. This little group rebelled especially against Simon McTavish. McTavish was becoming too much "the emperor". He wasn't giving the younger men a chance.

Perhaps their charges were true. McTavish had come a long way from the days when he personally grappled with the details of the fur trade. The very qualities which had enabled him to build up a great company under pioneer conditions made it difficult for him to share control. The little group of young men sought Mackenzie's advice, and finally broke away. They formed the New North West Company, soon known as the X.Y. Company. They built a depot half a mile from the Nor'Westers' Grand Portage—and quickly roused McTavish's ire. He was furious when he heard that Alexander Mackenzie had been friendly with the new group. For some time Mackenzie's growing importance had irked McTavish. When the company's agreement with its partners came up for renewal in 1799, McTavish ruled that Mackenzie shouldn't be re-elected. The ruling shocked every wintering partner in the great hall at Grand Portage.

"Drop Alexander Mackenzie!" they stormed, "Why, he's our strongest man!"

That further roused McTavish. Mackenzie, rather than cause dissension in the company, resigned, and his place was taken by Roderick, now Mrs. McTavish's brother-in-law.

Mackenzie had long wanted to write an account of his travels. At last he was free to do so. He retired to England, and when his *Voyages* was published in 1801 he immediately became famous. The Duke of Kent, Queen Victoria's father, had met him in Canada and was already a friend. Through Kent, Mackenzie met many of the most influential people in England and Scotland. In 1802, King George III knighted him.

But Sir Alexander was soon back in Canada. The X.Y. Company begged him to join them. Already they were cutting into the trade of the old North West Company, and McTavish had admitted that "the threatened opposition has become a formidable fact".

With Sir Alexander Mackenzie leading the X.Y. Company, the Nor'Westers found themselves up against a truly formidable foe. But they had faced—and crushed—opposition before. Arrogantly they called the X.Y. Company people "potties"— small measures. As the X.Y. Company, well financed by Mackenzie, sent hundreds of gallons of rum into the Indian country, the old company sent more. Where the X.Y. built trading-posts on locations unoccupied by the old company, the

Nor'Westers followed and built nearby. And since the Hudson's Bay Company was slowly expanding, the struggle for pemmican and pelts became three-way. Here and there free-traders added to the strife. Bitterness and hardship led to violence that flared up from Grand Portage to the most remote trading-posts.

Nor'Wester Alexander Henry, the Younger, heard, at his post, that the X.Y. people had told their Indians to kill him. Henry decided to take the natives by surprise before they could get together in strength in case the rumour was true. He intercepted small bands of Indians taking their pelts to the X.Y. post, and took the pelts by force from the women who were hauling them. The X.Y. people planned revenge, because they had already provided those Indians with shot and guns.

Up the Saskatchewan River the bitter struggle came to a head. On the prairies traders of all three companies had often travelled together for protection against the Blackfoot and Plains Crees, who had become offensive with so much rum. So, in the fall of 1802, an X.Y. Company clerk named La Mothe accompanied Nor'Wester James King on a trip to collect pelts from a band of Blackfoot out on the prairies. They travelled together like young men on business anywhere, in a friendly manner. But at the Indian camp the cordial relations ceased. La Mothe seized one lot of pelts which King claimed belonged to the North West Company.

"Would you give 'em up if you already had them in your hands?" charged La Mothe.

"No!" admitted King.

"Then I won't either," retorted the X.Y. man. "And don't force me to do something I don't want to do." La Mothe had a gun in his hand. It went off accidentally, he claimed later, and another man was killed in a fur-trade quarrel.

Meantime Simon McTavish was taking strong measures to meet opposition from the X.Y. "potties". To prevent other partners who might follow Sir Alexander Mackenzie's lead, he put through a regulation forbidding members to join in competitive trade, with a fine of £5,000 for each share held in the North West Company as a penalty. He leased for a twenty-one-year period the profitable territory along the Saguenay River held in French days as a royal monopoly and known as the King's Posts. He built a boat, *The Beaver*, and sent it into Hudson Bay to trade right under the eyes of the English company. And he outmatched the X.Y. Company in rum. Indeed, in 1803, the North West Company shipped over sixteen thousand gallons of rum to the northwest; well diluted with water, it was known by William McGillivray's term, "Blackfoot milk".

Accustomed to using strong methods, McTavish refused to listen to less extreme partners who insisted that the present struggle had become even more ruinous than the earlier struggle with Gregory, McLeod & Co. He scorned advice that the British Government was seriously concerned over debauching Indians in the northwest with rum, and violence such as had led to the death of young King. He was deaf to public opinion in Montreal. He was waging the fight with all his determination, and at the same time building a fine mansion on the slope of Mount Royal, when he collapsed and died in Montreal. He was only fifty-four.

The violent opposition between the two Montreal companies ceased with McTavish's death. His nephew, William

McGillivray, succeeded him. Within a few months the X.Y. Company rejoined the Nor'Westers, its partners receiving a quarter interest in the North West Company.

Sir Alexander Mackenzie organized a separate company to look after his private interests, took up bachelor apartments in Montreal with William McGillivray, and became Member of Parliament for Huntingdon. But in 1808 he returned to Scotland, married his beautiful Scottish cousin, Geddes, and prepared to settle down on a handsome estate.

Almost at the same time another wedding took place in Scotland. Thomas Douglas, Lord Selkirk, married Miss Jean Wedderburn-Colvile, the heiress to a large block of Hudson's Bay Company stock. Selkirk had read Mackenzie's *Voyages*. Keenly interested in settlement in North America, he had applied to the British Government for permission to found a colony for dispossessed Highlanders along the Red River. The British Government had advised him to seek a more suitable location. But Sir Alexander Mackenzie strongly suspected Selkirk's intentions. Mackenzie well knew the disastrous effects of Mississippi settlement on the southwest fur trade. He lost no time in urging William McGillivray to buy a controlling interest in the Hudson's Bay Company.

8

Fort William

*T*he struggle with the X.Y. Company and the threat from Lord Selkirk's interest in the Hudson's Bay Company weren't the only major problems faced by the Nor'Westers at the beginning of the nineteenth century. At last the boundary between the United States and British North America had been negotiated. West of Lake Superior it was to be the Pigeon River waterway and the 49th Parallel. No one knew what streams and lakes the 49th Parallel crossed, and no one cared very much at the time. But the Nor'Westers knew where the Pigeon River flowed, and cared greatly. It flowed into Lake Superior north of Grand Portage. Their inland capital, the northwest centre of their vast fur trade empire, was on American soil.

At the summer meeting of 1796—back before the X.Y. Company had been organized—one urgent item of business had topped the regular agenda: Where should the North West Company build its new depot?

Everyone talked about the location of the new post. The pork-eaters discussed it about their evening fires. So did the northmen, across the creek. Every guide—and no one knew the country as well as they—had his own idea as to the best site. *Bourgeois* and wintering partners returned to the topic again and again, seated by the fire on a cool evening, at meal-times, and, of course, at regular business sessions under the chairmanship of William McGillivray. In all the talk everyone agreed on three points: the new post must be on British soil—otherwise the United States could collect customs on all goods coming down from and going to the northwest; it must be on Lake Superior so that supplies could continue to be shipped by way of Sault Ste. Marie; and it must link with the old Rainy River-Lake of the Woods route.

But first a new route linking Lake Superior with the old route must be discovered. That job fell to Roderick McKenzie. "Roddy" spent most of two years seeking an ideal route. There was none. Though he explored stream after stream flowing into Lake Superior from the northwest, and north of the Pigeon River, he could find none without a very steep carry from the lake. The best was the old French route starting from the mouth of the Kaministiquia River. It wasn't as easy a carry as the Grand Portage—and that had been bad enough. Indeed, the French had abandoned the mountainous carry above the Kaministiquia River mouth and below Kakabeka Falls because of the hard climb. But it met the other requirements. Following the Dog and Savanne rivers, Sturgeon Lake and Maligne River, it rejoined the old route at Cross Lake.

The new capital, the Nor'Westers decided, must be more than just another Grand Portage.

"We will build a capital worthy of the North West Company," the proud partners agreed.

The new post must meet the greatly expanded needs of the company's greatly expanded trade. Now their empire stretched from the King's Posts on the Lower St. Lawrence to the Pacific Ocean and from the Upper Mississippi to the Arctic—a virtual monopoly of half of the continent but for the Hudson's Bay Company.

The new post cost well over £50,000. At times more than a thousand men worked on it. They built a palisade fifteen feet high, and large enough to encompass a good-sized village, with a gallery running round the top and a bastion at the southwest corner. The post's main gate faced the majestic height of Mount McKay. The Sleeping Giant and other rocky islands in the lake protected the east flank from the worst of Superior's storms. On the deep, protected shore of the Kaministiquia River a substantial dock berthed high-prowed Montreal canoes and a growing fleet of lake boats. To the west, on the flats, a vegetable garden provided the fort's potatoes and turnips; oats were grown and cattle grazed. By early summer of 1804 the new post was all that Grand Portage had been, and much more. The main building was larger and more imposing. Like everything else except the stone magazine, it was built of great peeled logs, stained brown. A gallery ran along the front of its two rows of windows. The great hall—sixty feet by thirty—occupied the centre of the building, flanked on one side by private rooms for the agents or senior partners when in residence, and on the other side by the steward's quarters. Soon paintings adorned the walls—among them a lifesize portrait of Lord Nelson and a scene depicting the Battle of the Nile. Pieces of statuary ornamented the mantels of the two great fireplaces; they included a handsome bust of Simon McTavish in the place of honour. Kitchens and servants' rooms were in the semi-basement. Clerks and interpreters stayed in log houses flanking the main building. And, to north, east and west ranged rows of buildings essential to the great industry of the fur trade: blacksmiths and tinsmiths; cooperages to make small kegs for the rum now shipped up by *bateaux* from Detroit; carpenter shops; and a well lit counting-house. The first doctor west of the Great Lakes lived in a log house near the main gate, not far from the popular pub, the *cantine salop*, where newly arrived pork-eaters and northmen met for their treat of fresh meat and bread and rum. There was, too, a jail—the *pot au beurre*, or butter tub, the *voyageurs* called it—where unruly young men cooled off after some of the worst brawls.

Now ships and canoes were built in well-equipped yards on the river front. Along the shore pork-eaters slept under their canoes, northmen pitched their weathered tents, and Indian bands put up their teepees much as they had done at Grand Portage. Every man—and every building—was there because of the wealth in pelts stored and sorted in newer and larger warehouses than the company had ever had. Yet even the warehouses were used only for a brief summer season. For a couple of months the £50,000-post with its luxurious accommodation and its expensive services sprang to life. For the rest of the year, as Grand Portage had been, it was left to a few caretakers.

Simon McTavish had come less frequently to the summer meetings toward the end of the eighteenth century. By the time the new depot was completed his nephew, William McGillivray, presided. After McTavish's death McGillivray became its chief executive, and the great new fort was named for him—Fort William.

The meeting following union of the X.Y. people with the North West Company was a proud occasion for William McGillivray. Within its twenty-five years the Montreal company had gained virtual control of the fur trade of all of what is today Canada except the Maritime Provinces. That year a single share of its stock sold for £4,000 and the company's returns were upwards of £200,000. As usual, the partners gathered in the sumptuous new great hall voted to distribute the year's earnings. Some wanted to build mansions in Montreal, others had already built fine houses or bought seigniories and wanted to enjoy them in affluence. None of the profits were put back into the company. The Nor'Westers never had bothered about a reserve fund. They had always been able to earn money. They had united the best fur-traders in the world, including some who must have been sorely missed by the Hudson's Bay Company. Why should they start saving now?

From their new capital the Nor'Westers faced the nineteenth century proudly, and arrogantly. Sir Alexander Mackenzie was back among them. Only a few years before, the Hudson's Bay Company's competent geographer, David Thompson, after fourteen years of service, despairing of ever becoming an explorer, had resigned and had become a partner in the North West Company; already they were making plans for him to explore a fur-trade route to the Pacific. The other new partner, Daniel Harmon, was being particularly successful at trading pemmican at the prairie posts. In Montreal, McGillivray maintained the standard of elegance established by his uncle. Montreal itself boomed on the wealth produced by the fur trade. Distillers made fortunes providing liquor for what was still the colony's only major industry. Streets of new houses sprang up on profits from handling pelts or importing trade goods. In England and even in the United States manufacturers prospered on the riches that came from trapping beaver and marten, otter and fox and less valuable fur-bearing animals in the still remote northwest.

Only a few free-traders were enterprising and courageous enough to attempt competition with the powerful Montreal fur barons. They were men very like the Nor'Westers themselves, men who believed in freedom to travel the linking maze of waterways, men who believed that they had a right to trade and even to trap if they had the initiative to do so. But the Nor'Westers had other ideas about rights in the northwest.

If a good man wanted to join the northwest fur trade, he could probably get employment with the North West Company. Otherwise he faced ruin. The Nor'Westers had developed the old French trade above Lake Superior. They had reached the Saskatchewan River in spite of hostile natives while the Hudson's Bay Company had made little attempt to explore even the streams covered by its alleged monopoly. They had pressed far beyond the limits bestowed by the charter of 1670—Peter Pond to cross Methye Portage ahead of any other white man; Sir Alexander Mackenzie to discover the way to the Arctic and to the Pacific; David Thompson already on the Upper Saskatchewan and about to probe the Rockies for a passage. The northwest was theirs by right of exploration.

They had done all this at great cost in money and much greater cost in their own individual courage and hardship and enterprise. They had taken the risks, and now they weren't going to let any man who could get together a canoe-load of trade goods reap their profits. Those who tried could expect similar treatment to that meted out to Dominic Rosseau.

In 1806 Rosseau got as far as the north shore of Lake Superior with a canoe-load, mostly trinkets he hoped to sell to *voyageurs* for their women. Carefully avoiding Fort William by roundabout streams and difficult carries, he finally put his canoe into a stream northwest of the fort, and his men paddled off to meet their prospective customers. One day they met a small group of Nor'Westers who warned Rosseau to go no farther. Rosseau retorted that they couldn't bully him. But he had only travelled a short distance farther when freshly fallen trees jammed the stream. He cleared these away. More trees, also freshly fallen, checked progress within the next few miles. And then great logs blocked the next portage. His progress was finally completely stopped. The party of Nor'Westers whose business it was to discourage free-traders repeated their warning. Rosseau took his goods back to Fort William where the North West Company bought them—at what they had cost in Montreal. Still having to pay his canoemen's wages, Dominic Rosseau returned to Montreal, there to spread the bitter news that the rule of Fort William was no myth.

David Thompson, Geographer

*T*he proud boast of the northern canoemen rang through the entire North West Company: *"Je suis un homme du nord!"* And in the northwest that was just another way of saying they'd rather be found dead than working for the Hudson's Bay Company.

Merely seeing some of the English company's Orkneymen trying to handle a canoe made the northmen swagger. Indeed, the Orkneymen actually seemed to prefer one of their slow, cumbersome York boats to a canoe! They had no rum, and little brandy for a *régale* at the end of a long, arduous day. They never had enough tobacco. No clerk ever had a chance of promotion to partnership in the Hudson's Bay Company. Truly these servants must be men of little spirit, content to work anywhere in Rupertsland, as they called the northwest, with only the bleak shores of Hudson Bay for a holiday.

Only rarely did one of the English employees stand head and shoulders above his plodding fellows to catch the Montrealers' attention. Older Nor'Westers still talked about Samuel Hearne, and now toward the end of the eighteenth century, there was David Thompson.

For several years parties of Nor'Westers had been aware of the Welshman, Thompson. They had met him surveying the boggy muskrat country of the Lower Saskatchewan; they had come across him at the prairie posts where the English company was slowly learning to trade pemmican, and at the headwaters of the Churchill River. On more than one occasion they had learned that Thompson was a good trader as well as being a competent surveyor. Indeed, the man had a way with the Indians, in spite of having little rum. During the winter of 1796–97 Nor'Wester Simon Fraser got to know the Hudson's Bay Company employee well. That year both Fraser and Thompson traded for their respective companies at Reindeer Lake, midway between Lake Athabasca and York Factory. A friendship, rare between men of the opposing groups, developed.

During the long winter Fraser found Thompson willing to talk about himself and his affairs, as Hudson's Bay people seldom talked.

David Thompson's father had died when Thompson was a baby, and he had been sent to the Grey Coat School at Westminster, "an institution designed to educate poor children in piety and virtue". There had been little kindness or affection for the little boy of seven. Perhaps it was this lack of affection which turned his interest to books of travel at an age when other children were playing games. By the time he was fourteen he had read *Mechanics*; *A Treatise of Algebra*; *Epitome of Navigation*; and *A Survey of the Tides*. The year he was fourteen the Hudson's Bay Company applied to the Grey Coat School for four boys with some knowledge of navigation for their posts in Rupertsland. Only two qualified, and one of those ran away to escape what seemed like banishment to Hudson Bay. David Thompson alone was signed on, and the company paid the school £5 for taking "the said boy appren[ce] for seven years".

Young Thompson spent his first year in America under Samuel Hearne at Fort Prince of Wales. The second year wasn't as fortunate. He was sent down to York Factory under Humphrey Marten who after twenty-four years on Hudson Bay had become as hard and cold as the country itself. But though Marten ruled with an iron hand, he taught the lad how to write up accounts and how to hunt. After a couple of years, Thompson journeyed inland to the Upper Saskatchewan, and helped to build Manchester House. Even then he dreamed of becoming an explorer. He got to know the Athabasca country while trading against the Nor'Western Frobisher brothers. He kept a meteorological journal, and with his simple equipment of compass and sextant he located the position of Cumberland House; that made Cumberland House one of the few points on the continent whose position on the earth was accurately known. Philip Turnor taught him surveying. Soon, he hoped, he would do some real exploring.

Two or three times the English company ordered him off exploring, but each trip ended only in trading. After a truly heart-breaking disappointment—he had been told to find a route between the Churchill River and Lake Athabasca, only to find that no canoes or food had been supplied—he took the matter in his own hands. He built his own canoe and hunted for game along the way. That was the most difficult trip of his entire association with the Hudson's Bay Company, but he succeeded in locating a route, through Reindeer and Wollaston lakes to the east end of Lake Athabasca. This first successful exploration, of great value to his company, brought him no reward. But it did bring him to Reindeer Lake and Simon Fraser's log house.

That year Thompson was due to sign on for another seven-years' term—he had already been with the company for fourteen years. He had travelled more than nine thousand miles of waterways, making surveys of over three thousand miles. His salary was only £60 a year, and he had no hope that the Hudson's Bay Company would ever give him a chance to explore.

"Join the North West Company," Simon Fraser advised the quiet Welshman with his dark hair cut in a heavy bang above his dark eyes. "You'll get plenty of opportunity with us!"

When spring came David Thompson accompanied Fraser down to the Montrealers' depot, then still at Grand Portage. The Nor'Westers received him royally, and quickly gave him the chance Fraser had promised. Indeed, he was the very man they needed. They put him to work at once—exploring and surveying the 49th Parallel, the boundary west of the Lake of the Woods.

The Nor'Westers exulted over the former Hudson's Bay employee, and Thompson set out happily on a great circle west to the Red River, and the Mandan Indian posts on the Missouri River and back to the headwaters of the Mississippi—which he called the Missouri—to the site of today's Duluth and right along the south shore of Lake Superior to Sault Ste. Marie. By the time he was back at Grand Portage he had covered some four thousand miles on foot, by canoe, on horseback and on snow-shoes. He proudly reported having taken positions all along the way, observing weather conditions, Indians, plants and animals. And all with only a ten-inch-radius sextant, a telescope, drawing instruments and a couple of thermometers.

During the brief summer meeting his fellow Nor'Westers got to know him better. Though his stern Grey Coat School upbringing had taught him never to drink, and he was the only man in the fort who regularly said his prayers, they liked his quiet manner. Best of all they discovered that he could tell stories with a poet's sensitive imagination. Many a pleasant evening slipped by with a group of partners and clerks listening to the quiet Welshman whose face was like that of Bunyan. As Dr. J. J. Bigsby, his partner on the International Boundary Commission, said, he could "create a wilderness and people it . . . or climb the Rocky mountains with you in a snow storm so clearly that you could shut your eyes and hear the crack of a rifle or feel snow flakes on your cheeks."

But much as the Nor'Westers needed Thompson's services as an explorer, they also needed him as an experienced fur-trader. For now the Hudson's Bay Company was putting up much stronger opposition. Perhaps losing Thompson had roused them, the Nor'Westers boasted. They elected him to partnership and put him in charge of the Athabasca country. Thompson did a good winter's trade, and while taking the pelts east stopped at Ile à la Crosse long enough to marry Charlotte Small, a Métis girl of fourteen. He made a note of the event in his carefully written journal, along with notes about the weather and local trade conditions: "This day married Charlotte". This day was June 10, 1799.

Now he went to new country far up the Saskatchewan River, to Fort George and Rocky Mountain House.

Ever since Alexander Mackenzie's great trip to the Pacific, the Nor'Westers hoped to find a satisfactory trade route through the Rockies. Simon Fraser had made his incredibly arduous exploration of the river bearing his name. But the Fraser was far too difficult and dangerous for canoes laden with trade goods and pelts. Surely, the Nor'Westers hoped, the Columbia, Vancouver's river, would prove to be more passable. Duncan McGillivray had already made one attempt to reach the headwaters of the Saskatchewan from which there was believed to be a pass to the Columbia, but he had been turned back by Piegan Indians. At last, David Thompson was to set out on a trip as challenging as any he had ever pictured in his dreams. He was to explore the Columbia River.

It was the spring of 1806. He had spent several years in the vicinity of Rocky Mountain House. Winter after winter he had managed the fur trade, taking the pelts down with the brigades each summer. He had asked questions of the natives, as Pond and Mackenzie had done earlier. He had made charts showing the results of his inquiries. And whenever he had a moment to spare—or to dream—he had spent it looking to the west and a gap in the Rockies. Through that gap, the natives had told him, emerged the Saskatchewan River. David Thompson figured that if he followed the Saskatchewan to its source, he would be close to the Great Divide. Surely, up there, he would find a stream flowing westward into the Columbia.

By 1806 the Hudson's Bay Company had expanded greatly. It had built many posts inland, and many of them were close to Nor'Wester posts. There were even indications that the English company might be considering a venture similar to that planned by the Montrealers. So David Thompson made his final plans with great secrecy. He was determined that his former associates should not reach the Columbia before him. The North West Company which had given him his great opportunity should be there first, as they had been first with Alexander Mackenzie to the Arctic and with Mackenzie and Fraser to the Pacific.

Thompson's young wife, Charlotte, went along, and their two babies. For he didn't know how long the trip would take, or when he might return. At first the going was easy. The Saskatchewan was broad and swift. But as the little party neared the mountains, the river flowed faster. Here and there they had to portage. At places the going seemed impossible, so steep were the climbs, so rugged the rocky river banks, so dense the undergrowth. In all his thousands of miles of canoe travel Thompson had seen nothing to compare with these jagged mountains, ever steeper and less hospitable, ever colder as he neared the patches of snow that hadn't melted by late June. Sometimes it seemed that the little party must reach the very mountain tops before they came on a pass. The Saskatchewan narrowed, its waters a white cascade. It became a mere trickle, icy and impassable. All around stretched miles of glaciers, never before seen by a white man.

David Thompson sensed that the great moment had come, even before he finally located a tiny stream flowing to the west. At last he was on the height of land, the Great Divide. Devout man that he was, he dropped to his knees and prayed that God would grant that he might follow the tiny stream flowing west, right to the Pacific Ocean, and return in safety. His prayer was answered. He was the first white man to explore the Columbia to its mouth.

For several years Thompson traded along and explored the Columbia's rich fur-bearing tributaries, though not the one bearing his name, the Thompson. The Hudson's Bay Company followed for a brief period but soon abandoned the vast pacific slope to the Nor'Westers. Steadily and completely Thompson developed the Rocky Mountain fur trade, along with his explorations, and he did both with very little liquor reaching the natives.

John MacDonald of Garth, in charge of Rocky Mountain

House when Thompson set out to explore the Upper Saskatchewan, had insisted that Thompson take a couple of kegs of rum with him. Thompson was determined that the fur trade would be carried on without rum, and without drunken Indians. He wrote an account of what happened in his *Narrative*: " . . . when we came to the defiles of the mountains, I placed the two Kegs of Alcohol on a vicious horse; and by noon the Kegs were empty and in pieces, the Horse rubbing his load against the rocks to get rid of it . . . I wrote to my partners that I would do the same with every Keg of Alcohol."

Thompson was doing all he could to keep down the cost of the long trip from Montreal, through Fort William to the Pacific. Eliminating rum—west of the Rockies—helped. So did his efforts to find the easiest passes. There was another important aspect of the Pacific trade which he kept always in mind. The North West Company had had to abandon Grand Portage at great cost because it was found to be on American soil. Thompson took all territory he discovered west of the Rockies in the name of Great Britain. When he built a new post he gathered together the Indian bands and his own men, raised the flag and publicly proclaimed the territory as belonging to British North America—and the North West Company. Before he finally retired he had visited—and claimed—most of today's Idaho, Washington, Oregon and Western Montana.

In 1812—after twenty-eight years in the northwest without once visiting civilization other than Grand Portage and Fort William—Thompson took his longest single canoe trip. With Charlotte and his already large family he crossed the Rockies and travelled by way of the Athabasca and Upper Churchill rivers to the Lower Saskatchewan and Lake Winnipeg. Pausing briefly at Fort William, he continued right down to Montreal. He never returned to the far northwest.

Thompson went to live at Terrebonne, to make the first map of the northwest third of the continent for the North West Company. When he had arrived on Hudson Bay, the North American continent was merely a vast expanse of white paper between Lake Superior and Captain Vancouver's Pacific coast. The only maps were Hearne's sketch of the Coppermine River and Peter Pond's rough map. Thompson's map—most of which depicted territory he had visited himself, located for the Nor'Westers and for posterity the great waterways and lakes and mountains of the northwest and the position of each in relationship to the others. When the map was finally completed, it was taken to Fort William. There with ceremony it was hung in the great mess hall, where it covered almost the entire end wall. For years it was a priceless source of interest and information, and a guide in planning the company's trade. It is now in Ontario's Provincial Archives, along with the thirty-two beautifully hand-written volumes kept by Thompson on his travels. Together the map and journals showed the North West Company the extent of the empire it controlled right across the territory claimed by the Hudson's Bay Company monopoly. As a result of this map both the American and British governments became aware of how vast a territory each might own. At the time, though, few were aware of the contribution of David Thompson, a great fur-trader, a Nor'Wester by choice, and one of the world's greatest geographers.

Lord Selkirk Opposes

When William McGillivray heard from Sir Alexander Mackenzie of Lord Selkirk's plan he couldn't believe it. A Hudson's Bay Company settlement on the Red River! Thousands of emigrants shipped from Scotland by way of Hudson Bay, the Nelson River and Lake Winnipeg, settlers on a vast tract of land astride the Nor'Westers' only link with its valuable Athabasca and Pacific trading areas! The scheme was fantastic. For three very obvious reasons the Nor'Westers must prevent it; first, because settlement would ruin the northwest fur trade as it already had done along the Upper Mississippi; second, because it would bring terrible suffering to the emigrants themselves; and finally, because it would deprive the Métis of their squatters' rights.

McGillivray remembered Thomas Douglas, Lord Selkirk, who had visited Montreal a few years earlier. Montreal had feted the engaging man in his early twenties; everyone had enjoyed meeting the educated, widely travelled young earl, still handsome in spite of the flush of early consumption, the disease which had apparently carried off his father and his six older brothers. The Nor'Westers had entertained him at dinner at the Beaver Club, the highest honour Montreal could pay any man.

Selkirk had greatly enjoyed that evening, as indeed he might. All the members wore their great gold medals bearing the motto "Fortitude in Distress" which were awarded only to men who had wintered in the *pays d'en haut*. The Beaver Club's finest beaver-monogrammed plate and glass were used and its most famous dishes served. There had been bear, beaver-tail soup, roast beaver and pemmican—all brought from a great distance at great cost for the event. And, of course, the finest of liquors. Selkirk had arrived with the earliest guests at four in the afternoon, drunk his bottle of wine with the married members, and stayed on after they left to drink their health till four in the morning. What a night it had been!

More than one Nor'Wester had danced a reel on the table between the cutlery the night they feted Selkirk. They had all sung until they were hoarse. Finally, before the party broke up, they'd treated him to the *grand portage*. The *grand portage* marked the very peak of such evenings: senior partners, wintering partners, business men, clerks and guests—each armed himself with a make-believe paddle. They searched the place for pokers, tongs, swords or walking-sticks. Then with a mighty Indian war whoop and the bonniest of Highland hoots, they sat themselves on the floor in two long rows. Singing lustily, they paddled an imaginary *canot-du-maître* with great gusto across the carpet.

Selkirk had sung with them the old songs beloved of *voyageurs*—"A la claire fontaine", "Lisette", "En roulant ma boule". And of course they had answered all his questions about the fur trade. McGillivray and Rod McKenzie had even taken him up to Lachine to see the early brigades leaving for the northwest. Selkirk had chatted with many of the *voyageurs* themselves, and to the guides and wintering partners. Indeed, if he really had had plans for a settlement in the fur-trade country, he had gained the necessary information while a guest of the Nor'Westers, whom he now planned to attack so treacherously, and from reading Nor'Wester Alexander Mackenzie's *Voyages*.

McGillivray, as shrewd a judge of men as his uncle had been, had doubts about Selkirk's rumoured Red River plans coming to anything. Selkirk was given to grandiose ideas without having the practical knowledge or stamina to see them through. He had been grieved over the fate of his Highland clansmen dispossessed by the Highland Clearance Bill—as what Highland Scot wasn't!—but the British government had wisely advised him to seek a more suitable location than the Red River for his colonization scheme. He had already brought out three other groups of colonists—one to Prince Edward Island, two to Lake Erie. All were failures. In each case the colonists had suffered the worst hardships of pioneering. And each time Selkirk had been unequal to fulfilling his dreams. He had arrived too late to direct settlement on Prince Edward Island. Both Lake Erie areas were too swampy for immediate farming. And now he planned a fourth attempt on the remote Red River, where the Métis would surely resent settlers who might dispossess them of their little homes.

The Nor'Westers had faced many a desperate situation before but none more potentially dangerous than this. For several years they had been pressing for a route through Hudson Bay. In London, where the North West Company had an office and where it did most of its buying and selling, McGillivray and Sir Alexander Mackenzie had been buying Hudson's Bay Company stock, currently depressed because no dividends had been paid for several years. But in spite of the low price of the English company's shares, they had been unable to secure anything near a controlling interest. The controlling interest was in Lord Selkirk's hands, most of it acquired through his marriage.

With no consideration for the native-born Métis, he had persuaded the Hudson's Bay Company to grant him some forty-five million acres of land astride the Red River. For it he paid a token fee of a few shillings, and agreed to settle several thousand colonists within ten years. The threat McGillivray had been unable to believe was only too true.

Even one thousand white settlers, eager to farm the virgin prairie, would ruin the fur trade along the Red River. Because there was no other linking waterway between the east and the far northwest, settlement would cut the Nor'Westers' very life line. As for the settlers themselves, McGillivray knew well how bitterly they would be resented by the Métis, descendants of Nor'Westers and Indians; and unless Selkirk had greatly changed, there would be little preparation for their arrival in the country, which was much less hospitable than the locations of his other ventures.

Nip it in the bud! William McGillivray and his fellow Nor'Westers decided to attack the scheme right in Scotland. Selkirk, they soon learned, had engaged Colin Robertson, a disgruntled Nor'Wester who had resigned a few years before because he felt he hadn't been promoted quickly enough, and another Canadian, Miles MacDonnell, as his agents. While these two set about securing the colonists who would be expected to recoup the Selkirk family fortunes in the northwest, Simon McGillivray wrote a series of letters to the *Inverness Journal*, signing himself merely "A Highlander". These he addressed to the landless Highland families then being approached by Selkirk's agents.

In his letters to the Inverness paper, Simon McGillivray

pointed out the dangers and difficulties of the voyage to Hudson Bay. Then he continued: "This voyage I do not think they can possibly perform in the present season for the frost will be approaching before they can reach Fort York, where I fancy they must pass the winter where many will perish before the spring from excessive cold and from want of food . . ."

The letters discouraged many of the unhappy Highlanders, but Selkirk was carried away with his ambitious scheme. He made MacDonnell Governor of his Red River colony, and urged him to go on with the plan.

Simon McGillivray had known what he was writing about. Not till a year later did the first weary, hungry, dispirited little band of settlers reach the Hudson's Bay Company's Fort Douglas on the Red River. As McGillivray had predicted, they had had to winter on the bleak shore of Hudson Bay, short of food, with only such shelter as they could provide for themselves. Many died of scurvy before even starting the arduous trip inland by way of the Nelson River and Lake Winnipeg. So badly was the venture planned, that there was no shelter ready for the settlers when they finally arrived at the site of the proposed colony.

As William McGillivray had anticipated, and as his brother Simon had indicated in the *Inverness Journal*, the Métis and Indians lost no time in showing the colonists that they were unwelcome. In war-paint and head-dress, a band of natives rode down on the little straggle of tents on the very day of the colonists' arrival.

The Nor'Westers at Fort Gibraltar reluctantly accepted an invitation from Miles MacDonnell to attend the founding ceremony of Selkirk's colony. They stood by while he fired the six small cannon he had brought from York Factory and while he ran up the flag. In the months that followed the Nor'Westers even fed some of the most desperately hungry and clothed others whose coats and plaids had worn thin since they left Scotland more than a year before.

The project was turning out just as they had predicted, and the Nor'Westers lost no time in sending word of Selkirk's shocking negligence to Scotland. They gathered facts about the number who had starved to death during the first winter at Hudson Bay, of others who had starved the following winter at the Red River, and of the surviving colonists' pitiful struggles to cultivate the tough prairie turf with only garden hoes. But even with runners and express canoes, news travelled slowly in the early nineteenth century. By the time word of the Red River tragedy reached Scotland, Selkirk had already sent off another group of colonists. They and even a third group reached the Red River in the next three years, to find no food, no supplies, no shelter ready either at York Factory or at the Red River settlement.

Yet all along the Nor'Westers watched and waited. At the rate the settlers were dying, and at the rate Selkirk was able to recruit others, he couldn't possibly settle the thousands required by his agreement within ten years.

The arrival of the second small group had forced Miles MacDonnell to near desperate straits to provide food for them. With only hoes to till the ground, they had so far been able to produce little grain. Many were existing on wild roots and small game and even the help of individual Nor'Westers. The arrival of Selkirk's third party drove MacDonnell to real desperation.

As Selkirk's representative he held a warrant to govern the colony until civil government could be established. Using this authority, he issued a decree confiscating all food supplies in the area. At Fort Gibraltar the Nor'Westers couldn't believe the decree sent to them by MacDonnell. But there it was, down on paper, signed by Miles MacDonnell on behalf of Lord Selkirk who claimed monopoly to the very land on which Fort Gibraltar was built. Not only did MacDonnell confiscate all food in the colony, but he forbade any fur-trader to ship out a pound of meat.

But it was here that the Nor'Westers stored pemmican for their Athabasca and Pacific slope brigades. Since Peter Pond's time they had traded pemmican from the prairie Indians and stocked it ready for the up-going canoemen and traders. They put in supplies for the Métis about the post and their families. Obviously the decree was intended to ruin the North West Company.

Not only did MacDonnell forbid the Nor'Westers to ship a single bag of pemmican from the Red River, he even seized six hundred bags of pemmican from Brandon post on the Assiniboine River to feed his colonists. Word of the decree reached the partners at Fort William as quickly as an express canoe could be paddled and carried by the *voyageurs*, as outraged as their *bourgeois*. It didn't take the agent and partners at Fort William long to decide what to do. Now it was their own people or the colony who must go. If one group must starve, that group wouldn't be the Nor'Westers who had collected and paid for their supplies of pemmican. Nor'Wester Duncan Cameron was despatched to the Red River with an offer to the colonists: those who wished to leave would be given free transport to

Montreal, by the North West Company, together with a year's provisions and a grant of two hundred acres of land—well distant from the Red River.

Over a hundred unhappy colonists accepted the offer and the Nor'Westers took them east. But a few couldn't decide whether to trust Selkirk's promises or those of the North West Company. The fact that even a few settlers remained alarmed the Métis afresh. Fearful that they might lose their little homes and their strips of land fronting on the Red River they burned down a settler's shack here, destroyed a tiny plot of barley nearby. They had all but driven the remaining settlers to desperate escape when Selkirk sent out another governor, an arrogant, strong-handed army captain—Robert Semple.

Semple gathered the remnants of the colony together. He served notice on the Nor'Westers at Fort Gibraltar that they must vacate their forts on Selkirk's land. When Duncan Cameron refused to acknowledge the governorship, Semple arrested him, and sent him off to England by way of Hudson Bay. Cameron later sued Selkirk for illegal detention, and won damages of £3,000. But meantime Semple tore down the Nor'Westers' Fort Gibraltar and floated the timbers to the Hudson's Bay Company's Fort Douglas. When Colin Robertson arrived, at Selkirk's command, to help Robert Semple maintain order, resentment that had smouldered along the Red River flared to a blaze. Now the Métis determined to stop at nothing to safeguard their homes. They got together under Cuthbert Grant, a Métis employee of the North West Company, and mounting their horses, rode to the Hudson's Bay Company fort near Seven Oaks.

Robert Semple went out to meet them, demanding what they wanted.

"We want our fort!" cried Grant, referring to Fort Gibraltar.

"Then go to your fort!" retorted Semple. He reached to grab the bridle of Grant's horse. One of the Métis saw the move. Fearful that Grant might be taken prisoner, he fired his gun, hitting Semple. Suddenly, like a prairie fire, shooting blazed through the tall grass and brush near the Hudson's Bay Company's Fort Douglas. Semple's men rushed out to his support, not yet knowing that he was dead. Men fired at each other from behind the shelter of their horses, and from the poplar woods. All the smouldering fears of the Métis were loosed; they had only one thought: to defend their homes. Before the fighting ceased one Nor'Wester was dead. Twenty of Semple's men died with him, and others were taken prisoner and shipped to Fort William.

There was great rejoicing at Fort William when Duncan Cameron arrived with several prisoners and word that the colony was at last destroyed.

"Our life-line is free!" the partners cried, and throughout the depot every man took up the cry. No longer would the fear of starvation threaten northmen and wintering partners and clerks beyond Lake Winnipeg. The Nor'Westers could guarantee supplies for their own people. It was unfortunate that so many men had died at Seven Oaks. But the Métis had been there before Selkirk's settlers; they had the first right to security.

It was a great victory and the Nor'Westers celebrated boisterously. The celebrations were boisterous partly because of the rumours that kept reaching Fort William that summer. Every canoe brought fresh news, more rumours. At the moment when the Montreal traders were rejoicing over securing their life-line, word came that Lord Selkirk had arrived in Montreal with his wife and family, at last intent on looking after his colony's interests personally. Then came a rumour that Selkirk had got himself appointed a Justice of the Peace for Canada, and that he had engaged a private army of a hundred Swiss mercenary troops, *de Meurons*, under a Captain D'Orsonnens. Selkirk, according to other rumours, had bribed his mercenaries with promises of land to each man who settled on the Red River.

William McGillivray, busy with the heavy burden of the company's summer routine, kept close check on all the rumours, shocked that Selkirk would resort to using foreign troops to protect him on his visit to the Red River. Toward the end of the summer word came that Selkirk was at Sault Ste. Marie, with the hundred mercenaries and over a hundred *voyageurs* engaged for him by Miles MacDonnell in Upper Canada. The partners of the North West Company were not surprised when a great brigade of canoes swept across Thunder Bay, and Lord Selkirk set up his armed camp across the Kaministiquia River from Fort William.

The next morning Captain D'Orsonnens of the *de Meurons* appeared at the gate of Fort William with a message from Lord Selkirk. The Scottish earl demanded release of the prisoners arrested by the Nor'Westers at the Red River. McGillivray complied. A few hours later, after questioning the prisoners, Selkirk sent his captain back to Fort William, this time with nine soldiers. As a Justice of the Peace for Canada, Selkirk had issued a warrant for the arrest of William McGillivray himself.

McGillivray thought Selkirk must be mad. Coming to Fort William with a couple of hundred armed men to arrest the head of the North West Company in the company's own depot! Dumbfounded, McGillivray decided he'd better go over to Selkirk's camp to see what it was all about. With two partners, Dr. John McLoughlin and Kenneth McKenzie, he was paddled across the river.

"What right have you to assume the powers of the Governor of Upper Canada?" he demanded of Selkirk.

Selkirk, greatly fatigued by the unaccustomed exertions of the journey and by excitement and ill health, was in an hysterical mood. He ordered Captain D'Orsonnens to arrest the three Nor'Westers. Each protested vigorously. Who did Selkirk think he was? Did he actually believe that his monopoly covered Fort William, as well as country drained by streams flowing into Hudson Bay? They accused him of being a high-handed dictator, an invader of private property. Selkirk replied by enforcing the arrest and by despatching another and larger squad of mercenaries to Fort William with orders to arrest the remaining partners. They, too, demanded to know by what authority Selkirk dared send his foreign mercenaries to private property where the Nor'Westers held a licence to carry on the fur trade. Meanwhile, one of the partners ordered the fort gates closed. Before the men could do so, a bugle call from Selkirk's lieutenant brought up reinforcements. The remaining six partners at Fort William were hustled off to Selkirk's camp, prisoners.

They found Selkirk exhausted from all the excitement. By the time he had questioned his important prisoners, they were able to persuade him to let them return to Fort William for the night, on condition that they make no hostile move.

Such a night as that Fort William had never seen. The partners of the North West Company were indignant and furious. But they had no troops to withstand Selkirk's army. So they spent the night sorting their papers to prevent Selkirk getting private or trade records. Toward morning many of the company's valuable documents were feeding great flames in the mess hall, others were being carried out through a back gate and buried in the garden plots on the flats. A small supply of ammunition was also cached in the garden plots. Next day, when Selkirk, ill and irritable after a sleepless night, learned of the steps taken by the Nor'Westers, he ordered a complete search of Fort William. Finally he seized the entire fort, including all the remaining papers and documents he could find. Under a strong guard, McGillivray and the other North West Company partners were sent to Montreal to stand trial.

William McGillivray had little fear that he wouldn't be released as soon as he reached Montreal. Selkirk, he knew, was in no health to stand a trip to the Red River so late in the autumn, and would have to spend the winter at Fort William. While he was doing so, McGillivray and his fellow Nor'Westers would have ample opportunity to plan retaliation—with vengeance.

Through his *voyageurs* and wintering partners, trading much as usual because the season had been planned before Selkirk's invasion, William McGillivray heard that Selkirk had gone to the Red River after wintering at Fort William. McGillivray received many a scornful account of the "proud benefactor" gathering together the remnants of his wretched colony during the spring of 1817. Selkirk had stalked about the little settlement telling the settlers where to build a church and a school, a grist mill and bridges, allotting his *de Meuron* mercenaries tracts of the land he had received for a few shillings. His presence at the Red River was the one thing to make good the old Hudson's Bay Company monopoly.

Probably Selkirk realized that, in spite of making good the old monopoly, he was himself in a dangerous position. When he was ready to return to Montreal, he lacked the courage to go back through Fort William. Instead he travelled by way of the United States.

William McGillivray was ready for him, whichever way he returned to Montreal. McGillivray had warrants issued, and ready to serve on Selkirk as he crossed the border. The warrants charged Selkirk with stealing muskets at Fort William, with entering the post riotously, and with assault. The case occupied the courts at Sandwich (near today's Windsor, Ontario) and at York (now Toronto) for months and aroused bitterness throughout the colony. The main satisfaction for the Nor'Westers was the fine of £1,500 lodged against Selkirk "for false imprisonment of a North West Company partner at Fort William". As well, Colin Robertson and Miles MacDonnell were charged with destroying the Nor'Westers' Fort Gibraltar.

Selkirk countered with charges against the Nor'Westers. Fort Gibraltar, he maintained, had been built on property belonging to the Hudson's Bay Company by right of its monopoly. More serious were his charges over what he called the murder of Robert Semple. In the months following Selkirk's return to Montreal, charge after charge was laid against the North West

Company. Through them all Selkirk found it as difficult to get a conviction against the powerful Nor'Westers as it had been for the Nor'Westers to persuade the British Government to grant them rights to the use of the Hudson Bay ports. In spite of the support of the Hudson's Bay Company monopoly, the Nor'Westers won most of the lawsuits. But it was a costly victory. The expense of defending their position used all the Montreal company's current profits—and more.

As a result the Nor'Westers found themselves dangerously in debt. Each year now, profits from the far-flung trade lines between Montreal and the Athabasca and Pacific slope districts diminished because of improved Hudson's Bay Company trade methods—and the English company's shorter, cheaper Hudson Bay route. The Nor'Westers were in no position to face those stupendous legal costs. William McGillivray and his fellow Nor'Westers faced the grim truth: they must secure the right to ship through Hudson Bay or eliminate the Hudson's Bay Company.

"When Among Wolves, Howl!"

"That fickle traitor, Robertson!"

The Nor'Westers could scarcely find words strong enough to express their contempt for Colin Robertson. When the former wintering partner had resigned, complaining that he hadn't been promoted to full partnership quickly enough, the North West Company had given him a generous testimonial along with their sincere regrets. He had gone to England to start business on his own with the cordial wishes of his fellow fur-traders. Not until after Selkirk's invasion of Fort William had they grasped the magnitude of his disloyalty.

Only gradually had they pieced together Robertson's actions in London. He had gone into business, as he had planned. But very soon afterwards he had trotted round to the Hudson's Bay Company with an offer so preposterous that, at first, the English company hadn't taken him seriously. For what he had offered his former opponents was nothing less than the whole of his experience as a trader; he had offered to reorganize the conservative old company, even to the extent of engaging French-Canadian *voyageurs* and guides and interpreters in Montreal. He had actually urged the Hudson's Bay Company, with his help, to invade the rich Athabasca region discovered and explored by the Nor'Westers and completely outside the Hudson's Bay Company monopoly.

The Hudson's Bay Company had turned down the proposal, partly because it was much too ambitious for them, partly because they suspected a man who so easily changed his allegiance. But its shareholders were clamouring for dividends. Its stock was a drug on the market, as Sir Alexander Mackenzie and William McGillivray heard often both in London and Montreal. It was heavily in debt to the Bank of England.

Selkirk's Red River settlement was ample proof to the Nor'Westers that its shareholders had forced the Hudson's Bay Company to action—and acceptance of Robertson's plan. Every Nor'Wester knew the danger of a settlement astride the Red River. But to have the Hudson's Bay Company invading the Athabasca country was a challenge that must be met with everything they had—men, more trade goods, rum, and their bare hands if necessary. Colin Robertson's motto had been: "When you are among wolves, howl!" The Nor'Westers determined to show him—and the Hudson's Bay Company—that they, too, could howl. Indeed, they had probably taught Robertson all he knew about howling.

"Avoid force if you can," the partners at Fort William advised wintering partner Archibald Norman McLeod before he left to take charge of the Athabasca trade the year following Selkirk's reorganization of the Red River settlement. "But get the pelts!"

At Fort Chipewyan, Nor'Wester McLeod kept a close watch on John Clarke, whom Robertson had engaged to lead the Hudson's Bay Company's invasion of the Athabasca territory. He soon discovered that the English company hadn't yet greatly changed. Clarke had little rum. He was very short of provisions. And he wasn't a very astute fur-trader. As a former trader with John Jacob Astor's fur company, Clarke should have known better than to build several outposts to Fort Wedderburn when he had so little food. Instead, he sent his men long distances from his main depot. Anticipating what would happen, McLeod outfitted the Indian trappers, treated them to a little rum, and warned them not to trade with the invaders. If they did trade food or pelts with the English—no rum, no ammunition, no means of hunting food for themselves or their families!

Short of pemmican, Clarke's men turned to hunting game and fishing. Both failed. Soon they were desperately hungry, and the Indians refused to trade. One by one the English appealed to McLeod for food. The Nor'Wester agreed willingly—but at a price. After all, his company was now at war with the Hudson's Bay Company, and these men were invaders. His price was a promise from the English not to trade in the Athabasca territory for an entire year. Most agreed. A few stubbornly turned down the terms. That, decided Archibald Norman McLeod, was their own affair. No promise, no food. And let Clarke take the blame. Still trying to get along without aid from McLeod, Clarke attempted to recall his men to Fort Wedderburn where there was some fishing. But the season was already well advanced. The rivers froze. One group of sixteen was forced to abandon their canoes and tramp through the woods, without food and unable to find any game. Thirteen of them died on the way, dropping out one by one from exhaustion.

As the winter progressed, Clarke himself had to beg food from McLeod. He became deeper and deeper in debt to the North West Company. Finally, McLeod seized Fort Wedderburn. When Clarke protested, McLeod showed him a letter from William McGillivray giving an account of Lord Selkirk's seizure of Fort William. If that was the way the Hudson's Bay Company did business, the Nor'Westers would do likewise. As a Justice of the Peace for Canada—most senior partners held such authority to maintain order in the northwest—McLeod arrested Clarke. When spring came, instead of sending the Hudson's Bay man to Montreal for trial, McLeod sent him to Great Slave Lake, four hundred miles farther north. Without violence, he had ensured that Clarke would attempt no more illegal trade against the North West Company for the next year. And as he expected, Clarke's inept management led to his recall.

But if Clarke hadn't seriously cut into the Nor'Wester's trade, the mere presence of the Hudson's Bay Company had great nuisance value. Though the English had little to trade for pelts, the natives quickly sensed the bargaining value of two companies. And Clarke had assured them that Fort Wedderburn would be a permanent Hudson's Bay Company establishment. A few hopefully remembered the days when both the North West and the X.Y. companies had bargained for their pelts.

As soon as the ice left the rivers, McLeod took his canoe brigade down to Fort William. The year's trade hadn't greatly suffered, but he stocked up with an extra supply of rum to be prepared for whatever opposition the next season might offer. On his return to Fort Chipewyan his first news was that Colin Robertson himself was in charge over at Fort Wedderburn.

Robertson boasted of the large brigade of canoes he had brought to Athabasca, all manned by experienced French-Canadian *voyageurs*. He told every Nor'Wester who would listen of how he had put new life into the Hudson's Bay Company. He, Colin Robertson, had taught them to pack their canoes with a variety of goods so that there would still be an assortment of goods if one canoe should be lost; up till now the English company had packed each commodity—guns and ammunition, kettles, calico and blankets, knives and awls in separate canoes. He had advised the English to guard against starvation by clearing land and growing vegetables about its posts. He had even suggested an inland depot at the mouth of the Saskatchewan River on Lake Winnipeg, a sort of Hudson's Bay Company Fort William.

Archibald Norman McLeod heartily disliked Colin Robertson. He resented the man's presence in Athabasca territory, his swaggering manner, the way Robertson tried to impress the natives with his strength in man-power and in rum and tobacco. Already some of the Chipewyan Indians, hitherto loyal to the Nor'Westers, were shopping about from post to post for the largest gift of rum. Warily the Nor'Wester watched for a chance to use his authority as a Justice of the Peace. Sooner or later Robertson would swagger too much and carelessly make a slip. The chance came when Robertson boasted to the natives that he'd destroy Fort Chipewyan if the Nor'Westers gave him any trouble. McLeod issued a warrant, as insurance, and arrested Colin Robertson. The chief factor of the Hudson's Bay Company spent the next eight months a prisoner, lodged in a tiny shack out beside Fort Chipewyan's privy.

McLeod took care that no harm came to Robertson. He had plenty of food—he was allowed to receive whatever Fort Wedderburn could provide—and to some extent to supervise his company's affairs. When spring came, he was put in a canoe along with the brigade. Probably because he couldn't likely do much harm to the Nor'Wester's trade now the season was over,

McLeod allowed him to escape near Cumberland House. He hoped he'd never hear of him again, and continued his trip down to Fort William.

As they had done for years, other North West Company brigades came down the Saskatchewan one after another for several weeks, from the Pacific slope and from the Upper Saskatchewan. Each year it was much the same. The partners and some of the senior clerks got out of the canoes above Grand Rapids, the three-mile stretch of white water at the mouth of the Saskatchewan River, and strolled over the portage trail to await the canoes after they had shot the rapids. When the water was high this could be done without unloading the cargoes.

A week or so after Robertson's escape two Nor'Westers, John Duncan Campbell and Ben Frobisher, the latter a son of the original partner of the company, strolled along the familiar portage trail toward the wide expanse of Lake Winnipeg. This was always one of the pleasant parts of the trip. Brigades met, and news was exchanged. With spring in the air and the winter's trade accomplished, every man felt in a happy mood. Suddenly, taking them completely by surprise, a group of armed men rushed at Campbell and Frobisher from the bushes along the trail. The two were ordered to halt. Instinctively they resisted, when each was grabbed and his arms pinioned behind his back. Ben Frobisher was seriously wounded on the head with a gun butt.

As the two indignant Nor'Westers were forced along toward the end of the portage trail, Colin Robertson appeared. With him was William Williams, introduced to the two captive Nor'Westers as governor of the Hudson's Bay Company in

Rupertsland. Boastful as ever Robertson pointed out a small gunboat anchored in the lake, with a couple of cannon pointed up the rapids. That, said Robertson, had been his idea. He had also persuaded Williams to bring up a detachment of *de Meurons* from the Red River to prevent the Nor'Westers from using the portage.

During this series of announcements Frobisher had been obviously suffering from his head wound. But Campbell demanded to see the warrants for their arrest.

"I act upon the charter of the Hudson's Bay Company," Williams told them. "As governor and magistrate in these territories I have authority and will do as I think proper."

Williams also announced that he would act independently of "the rascally government of Canada", and make use of the colonists "to drive out of the country every damn Nor'Wester or perish in the attempt."

Campbell and Frobisher, lodged in a temporary jail on a tiny island, felt that Robertson now was truly howling like a wolf. Soon they were joined by other wintering partners and senior clerks, as Williams and Robertson ambushed each brigade. The tiny jail was crowded with indignant Nor'Westers. In vain they protested. It was a repetition of Selkirk's high-handed disregard for property at Fort William. All the *voyageurs* were permitted to go free, but the partners were taken by way of the Nelson River to Fort York and then to England. Only one escaped, Ben Frobisher. Suffering from his head wound, Frobisher wandered for days in the bush, without food, trying to reach the nearest North West Company post. He made a gallant attempt, but died only a short distance from it, weakened from the results of the blow from a Hudson's Bay Company musket.

Back at Fort Chipewyan in the autumn Archibald Norman McLeod found Robertson swaggering more than ever and boasting that at last the Nor'Westers were on the run. But he made little comment. All through the winter he went about his business, tight-lipped, and itching to get back at Robertson. Carefully he made no show of resentment, not even when he heard that Robertson had boasted that the Nor'Westers were afraid to protest.

That spring McLeod left early with his brigade, just as soon as the ice was out of the rivers. He was away well ahead of Robertson. But when he reached Grand Rapids portage, he didn't hurry on down Lake Winnipeg as usual. In spite of black-flies and mosquitoes, he waited. With him were several other wintering partners. Indeed, as the earliest Nor'Wester brigades came down, and as the partners heard McLeod's plan, each man eagerly consented to what would have been considered a waste of time any other year. They agreed to delay the tight fur-trade schedule. They were all waiting, having kept a steady watch, when Colin Robertson and his clerk finally appeared at the end of the portage trail. His canoe was shooting the rapids, and as usual, he was enjoying the stroll.

Suddenly, with a whoop, a group of Nor'Westers rushed at him from the bushes. They grabbed him without ceremony, and pinned his arms behind him. The louder he protested, the rougher they handled him. Now he was demanding to know by what right he should be treated in such a high-handed manner. How dare they waylay a leading servant of the Hudson's Bay Company? Archibald Norman McLeod and his fellow

Nor'Westers laughed grimly. Ben Frobisher had been not only the son of an original North West Company partner, but a popular and a competent fur-trader. They had little sympathy for the former wintering partner whose ambush had led to young Frobisher's death. As they hustled him off to the same little island jail where last summer he and William Williams had held the Nor'Westers, his own canoe came down the rapids. Robertson yelled to his canoemen to keep going, to hurry on to York Factory. Next day he was on the way to Montreal, demanding in vain to see the Nor'Westers' warrant for his arrest.

It was a triumphant moment for the Nor'Westers, lingering at the rapids at the mouth of the Saskatchewan, to watch the canoe bearing Colin Robertson grow small on the expanse of Lake Winnipeg. Surely the end of the struggle was in sight now. The Hudson's Bay Company's credit with the Bank of England was stretched to the limit; Lord Selkirk was desperately ill with consumption in the south of France, and Lady Selkirk was known to resent his personal concern with the details of trade. With Robertson out of the picture, they'd surely be free to trade in peace.

But the fur trade had already lost too much time this season. Quickly Archibald Norman McLeod rapped out an order. *Bourgeois* and *voyageurs* whipped into their various tasks. Everyone had enjoyed the counter-ambushing of Robertson. Soon the camp at the foot of Grand Rapids was breaking amid a rush of excited French. Laden canoes were pushed into the fast water at the river's mile-wide mouth. Steersmen and bowmen steadied canoes while gentlemen were carried to their places. The brigade headed for Fort William.

Well ahead of it, Colin Robertson hunched glumly down in the Nor'Wester canoe, wrapped in his bitter thoughts as the *voyageurs* sped him southeast instead of northeast to York Factory and Hudson Bay and England as he should be going. Everything had gone wrong for him. Knowing the Hudson's Bay Company could ill afford the loss of his services for the coming year, he felt that he had gained little by howling like a wolf. And then one day, far ahead, he saw a canoe brigade approaching. At first each canoe was a mere speck on the water's low horizon. But from the precision with which each canoe kept its position, from the speed with which the entire brigade shortened the distance between them, this was obviously a North West Company outfit. As Robertson's *voyageur* guards drew opposite the oncoming brigade, the men shouted greetings in quick, excited French. They asked and gave news. Soon Robertson recognized the *bourgeois*. Daniel Harmon, pressing on, no doubt, to some remote wintering place, recognized the former Nor'Wester. Across the wind-swept water he shouted a greeting. And then came the most fateful news Colin Robertson could hear: "Selkirk is dead!"

For a moment a shocked hush followed Harmon's news. Then, as the shouts of the passing brigade faded, Robertson's Nor'Wester *voyageurs* broke into a jubilant clamour of joy and relief. It was almost more than Robertson could bear. "Selkirk is dead!"

But whatever the news of Lord Selkirk's death meant to Robertson, it meant more to the wintering partners of the North West Company meeting at Fort William in the summer of 1820. That summer the wintering partners discussed the events of the past year or so among themselves. Each had felt for some time that he knew better than did the senior partners in Montreal the seriousness of the senseless struggle between the two companies. Even now, they couldn't pin McGillivray down to a plan for negotiating union. And now more than ever they were concerned about their savings in the company. How could the North West Company go on using so much rum, how could it continue that long haul from Montreal against the English company's shorter trip and increasing trade efficiency? Even the brief excitement of besting the English company at Grand Rapids seemed childish, and it had greatly delayed getting the pelts down to Fort William.

That summer the wintering partners held a secret meeting. They feared the effects of a split between the Montreal partners and themselves. But they feared the growing strife more. It was a desperate move, but they finally decided to approach the Hudson's Bay Company themselves. To do so they elected two of their members, Dr. John McLoughlin and Angus Bethune, to go to London to discuss terms of union.

12

"We Are Drowned Men…"

William McGillivray and his brother Simon sailed for England to negotiate with the Hudson's Bay Company, not knowing that the two representatives of the wintering partners were in London on a similar mission.

The McGillivrays were in a soberly optimistic mood. The North West Company was up against it, but so also was the Hudson's Bay Company. As everyone in business circles in London knew, the Hudson's Bay Company was heavily in debt; it owed the Bank of England, its supply houses and its employees, over £100,000. To discuss the two companies' mutual problems, the Montreal business men went to see Andrew Colvile, Lady Selkirk's brother, who had been conducting the English company's affairs during Lord Selkirk's illness and since his death.

The McGillivray's were willing to settle on an agreement similar to that which had united the X.Y. with the North West Company. The Hudson's Bay Company could contribute its monopoly, now fairly well established as a result of Selkirk's unhappy colony, and the port of York Factory on Hudson Bay. With these assets, the North West Company would become the greatest in the world.

They had talked about it often, both in Montreal as two of Canada's wealthiest and most influential citizens, and in London where they were also well known. They had often added up their real and hoped-for assets. The Nor'Westers' vast fur-trade empire, the territory their partners had discovered and explored, the business they had developed through the personal initiative and zeal of proprietors, wintering partners, clerks and guides, the *esprit de corps* of their *voyageurs*, all this and the Hudson's Bay Company monopoly—truly, it was a dream worthy of their efforts. What an era of peace, progress and prosperity could result to Canada from such a union. Both William and Simon McGillivray would have welcomed Sir Alexander Mackenzie's shrewd advice, his strong allegiance to the Montrealers' cause, but Mackenzie had died within a couple of months of Lord Selkirk, his end, like Selkirk's, hastened by worry over the bitter strife; no man had wanted union more than Alexander Mackenzie.

Already the McGillivrays had found the British Government keenly interested in union of the two companies. For some time it had been deeply concerned over troubles in the "Indian countries". Colonial Secretary Lord Bathurst had appealed to Edward Ellice, an outstanding London merchant, to see about the possibility of some sort of union. Ellice had long supplied the North West Company with trade goods, and was closely associated with its progress. He was also a member of parliament and a leader in the Whig party. For the latter reasons he was likely to be trusted by the shareholders of the Hudson's Bay Company.

William and Simon McGillivray found Andrew Colvile willing to discuss their mutual problems. For their part, they assured him that they could raise enough capital to continue the struggle, suicidal as it was becoming; they felt certain, however, that the Hudson's Bay Company was as eager as they to see an end of it. Colvile agreed that the strife was becoming suicidal. Though he wasn't completely sure that the Nor'Westers could raise funds to continue the struggle, he well knew the determination of its individual partners. Politely, but without apparent enthusiasm, he suggested that they meet again—later—for further discussions. And at each subsequent meeting William and Simon McGillivray sensed that he was stalling for time, trying to put them off. They soon discovered why.

The wintering partners—Dr. John McLoughlin and Angus Bethune—had been holding secret meetings with Andrew Colvile.

With the discovery that Dr. John McLoughlin and Angus Bethune had been meeting Colvile, William McGillivray knew that the tide had turned against the Nor'Westers. And it was of their own doing. Almost at the moment he learned of the two wintering partners' visit, he discovered that Colvile had been as desperate as he and his brother had been. Had the Nor'Westers remained united, they could have forced the hard-pressed directors of the Hudson's Bay Company to deal with them. Now it was too late. Their betrayal of each other's trust had permitted the English company to divide the Montreal company as sharply as Selkirk's Red River Colony had divided the fur trade.

Colvile was quick to take advantage of the split among the Nor'Westers. Adroitly he wedged the split wider, using the very characteristic which had enabled the Nor'Westers to build their vast empire—each man's strong individuality. One day he received the McGillivrays, the next the representatives of the wintering partners. Ruthlessly he played one faction against the other. For a time, through both sets of meetings, he seemed to favour the wintering partners. When it came to a final settlement between the Hudson's Bay Company and the Nor'Westers, he decided to deal with the senior partners, William and Simon

McGillivray; he astutely realized that they would likely set up another opposition if they were left out of any agreement.

For a year, while Dr. McLoughlin and Angus Bethune had taken word of their failure back to their fellow wintering partners, the sorry negotiations dragged on in London. In the Canadian northwest, in the dark about their fate, the men of the two great companies continued to struggle against each other, using fists and even weapons as well as their wits. Eventually, as spring came to London, the McGillivrays signed an agreement "on behalf of themselves and the North West Company of Montreal" and the Hudson's Bay Company. The wintering partners were to hear the terms of the agreement at the summer meeting of 1821.

They came to Fort William from every part of the far-flung fur-trade empire, from the Columbia and Fraser River territory, from the Peace and Athabasca and Mackenzie River systems, from the Upper Saskatchewan and Upper Missouri and the prairie posts, from the Lake of the Woods and Lakes Nipigon and Temiskaming, and from the King's posts along the St. Lawrence. Proud, but bewildered by the lack of details of what had taken place, they gathered in the great hall to hear those terms of union from William and Simon McGillivray and from a representative of the Hudson's Bay Company, Nicholas Garry. Quietly each took his place in the room where they had so often dined and danced and sung together, where they had cheered the news of Selkirk's defeat at the Red River, and cursed his invasion.

Under the amalgamation the name of the Hudson's Bay Company would continue, together with the rights of the old monopoly. That was good. Indeed, while the Nor'Westers would have greatly preferred to keep their famous name, the monopoly associated with that of the English firm meant more from a shrewd business angle. The two parties to the agreement would provide equal capital and divide the profits and losses equally. This brought murmurs of approval. The combined company would be run from London with a governor, appointed by the Hudson's Bay Company, and a board of four, two members from each. This wasn't so good. Why should the Hudson's Bay Company hold a balance of authority, demanded the men who had explored the vast country from Montreal to the Pacific and from the Upper Missouri River to the Arctic Ocean, the vast territory spread before them on David Thompson's magnificent map?

The hundred shares of the newly organized company provided that a percentage would be set aside for Lord Selkirk's heirs, for the McGillivrays' firm which had supplied the Montreal company, and for the shareholders of the English company. There would be a reserve fund built up from the profits of ten shares. Sitting tensely on the edges of their chairs, the wintering partners waited for details of the provision which affected each personally. What would they get out of the new deal? When the announcement finally came, its import dawned on them only after long, shocked moments. They were to have a block of shares—but shares in the current business not in the old London company. They were not to be partners under the amalgamation; instead they would merely be chief factors and chief traders in the new Hudson's Bay Company.

"Amalgamation!" cried the wintering partners of the North

West Company bitterly. "This is not amalgamation. This is submersion. We are drowned men!"

They recalled how union with the X.Y. Company had necessitated dropping many good men, for the simple reason that fewer were needed when opposition no longer had to be met. The same thing would happen again now. Who among them, they asked each other desperately, would be dropped, who have to seek strange occupation outside the only field for which he was fitted by experience or inclination? What of the clerks, the young men who had apprenticed themselves with the expectation of becoming partners? What of men who must serve at posts which had long been the scenes of bitter opposition with the old Hudson's Bay Company?

Slowly, fatefully, the Nor'Westers began to comprehend the price they were paying for their strong individualism. Had they remained united, they might have won much better terms, if not complete victory. A few fully realized how shrewdly Andrew Colvile had taken advantage of their divided negotiations.

But it was all over now. They had traded right across the territory shown on David Thompson's map, much of it far beyond the limits of the original Hudson's Bay Company charter of 1670. The new Hudson's Bay Company would control not only its old monopoly, but also the territory west of the Rockies, the finest beaver country on the continent, and the vast Mackenzie and Athabasca regions. And they who had been the discoverers, the explorers, would be allocated their future employment by deed poll. They who had conquered half a continent were no more. Fort William would give way to York Factory as the depot of the fur trade. Montreal's harbour would no longer buzz with the excitement of incoming and outgoing ships on fur-trade business.

William McGillivray watched the scene in the great hall throughout the long days of August, 1821, watched those tall proud Highlanders, who had made the North West Company great, file out for the last time, never to return to Fort William. When each had gone his way and the Nor'Westers had passed into history, McGillivray looked about the great hall named in his honour. He was a ruined man. But more than his own fortunes and hopes were ruined. Canada's first industry had suffered a crippling setback. Even the papers of the North West Company, the records of an era, would be shipped to the London headquarters. There was nothing for him to do but leave.

Broken, weary and dispirited, William McGillivray settled down in the high-prowed canoe which would take him back to Montreal. As each familiar landmark vanished from his sight, picture after picture flashed through his mind: Simon McTavish shaking sand on the wet ink of his signature at the bottom of the first real North West Company agreement, at Grand Portage in 1784; Alexander Mackenzie, older and more mature and with the look in his wide-set eyes of a man who has faced great odds and won, stalking up and down before the mess-room fire as he recounted the struggles of his trip to the Pacific; the proud satisfaction on the face of each man when the X.Y. and North West companies toasted union at the first meeting at Fort William; David Thompson poring over his map . . . Were they all to be remembered only as names on that map? Would nothing else remain of the vast empire they had explored—not even a page in history?

And, Afterwards...

Washington Irving wrote of them: "the lords of the lakes and forests are gone forever". Indeed the new Hudson's Bay Company swallowed their identity in its mammoth reorganization. For over a century their record lay untouched, forgotten in the archives of the old English company. For over a hundred years their exploits as individual men were overlooked. Families who had made Montreal great and prosperous disappeared as they sought new homes elsewhere, new lives. The very name of the northwest gave way to that of Rupertsland.

And yet those Nor'Westers were the transfusion which saved the Hudson's Bay Company. With the transfusion new blood, strong and vital and healthy, flowed into the old company. Men who had forcefully checked its progress now brought to it their shrewd knowledge of Indian trade, as well as the rich territory they had explored far beyond the limits of the ancient charter bestowed by Charles II. During the next fifty years when the Hudson's Bay Company virtually ruled from the Pacific to Labrador, many a former Nor'Wester or his son managed the fur-trade posts that dotted the wilderness like ancient feudal strongholds.

The vision and initiative of those Nor'Westers from Montreal, coupled with the efficiency possible under a real monopoly, and that short haul through Hudson Bay made the Hudson's Bay Company the greatest the world has seen. They were the men whose courage and enterprise and daring laid the foundation for Confederation. They inspired the very character of the Canadian people.

Index